Dedication

Inasmuch as this is the first (and most likely ONLY) book I have written, I feel compelled to uncharacteristically exercise some caution in dedicating it to anyone.

That said, I dedicate this book to Joe Allen of Joe Allen Restaurants www.joeallenrestaurant.com. Had he not asked one simple question back in 1982, I doubt I would have ever written anything. Through a terse exchange on his lawn, he challenged me to write. For almost thirty years I pondered that challenge. Things happen slowly in Vermont, but they get done after a while.

I further dedicate this book to my friend Jay Hathaway, who passed before the book was released. I know he would have said, "How cool is that."

Acknowledgments

Many thanks to the world's greatest political cartoonist, Jeff Danziger, for his generosity, wonderful talent, and friendship.

Thanks to Louis Porter for his input. Editing is hard enough on a well-written book. It took him forever but, fortunately, he was much faster at editing than I was at writing.

Thanks also to Frank Bryan, Evelyn Wilde Mayerson, and Don Hooper for their thoughtful comments and guidance.

Thanks to Ed Woods, who called me out in an editorial in the *Bennington Banner*, suggesting that I start writing a column. I am grateful to Ed and the *Bennington Banner* for allowing me a forum from which to spew out thoughts to the world twice a month.

Extra special thanks to Sandy Taylor who did a very thorough job in editing this book. She is the primary reason I don't sound like a complete moron. This was not an easy book to edit. She probably saved my marriage; for that I am grateful.

Lastly, I thank my wife, Alison, who notwithstanding would prefer that I do most anything else but waste time in front of a computer, doing useless things like writing a book that few will ever read, not only supports me in my various endeavors but on occasion encourages me to write.

How to Survive the
Recession
A Vermont Perspective

By Bob Stannard

SHIRES
PRESS

4869 Main Street
P.O. Box 2200
Manchester Center, VT 05255
www.northshire.com/printondemand.php

How to Survive the Recession
A Vermont Perspective
©2010 Bob Stannard
Illustrations ©2010 Jeff Danzinger

ISBN Number: 978-1-60571-058-7
Library of Congress Number: 2001012345

Building Community, One Book at a Time
This book was printed by the Northshire Bookstore, a family-owned, independent bookstore in
Manchester Ctr., Vermont, since 1976. We are committed to excellence in bookselling. The
Northshire Bookstore's mission is to serve as a resource for information, ideas, and entertainment
while honoring the needs of customers, staff, and community.

Printed in the United States of America

Contents

Introduction

Introduction

If you were born and raised in Vermont, then you know that our hay days were right after the Revolutionary War. Vermonters have assumed we've been in a recession since around 1790. The rest of the country is now catching up to us.

To quote my friend, Frank Bryan, "Think of Vermont as the slowest car in a stock-car race. After the race has been in progress for a while, there comes a time when the faster cars close in and are about to lap the slowest car. However, if you had gone to take a leak and got back to your seat just at that very moment, it would appear as though the slowest car is actually in the lead."

Vermonters have always considered themselves to be the leaders in just about everything from billboard laws to gay marriage. Recessions are no exception.

"Whenever a person dies, a library of stories dies with them."
James P. Stannard, Sr.

For thirty years or so people have said to me, "You ought'a write a book." Right. First, who has the time? Then, and perhaps this should have been first, who would want to read it?

For those of you who bought this book, I can't thank you enough. You might just have saved one more person from the unemployment lines, so you should feel better already. This might be a good place to STOP reading.

On the other hand, you've made it this far; you bought this book (or hopefully somebody did) and it's in your hands so you might as well put one foot in front of the other and begin the march of a thousand miles. Watch out for the rocks.

Chapter 1

The Meaning of Life

Before we solve the problems of living through a recession, perhaps it would be best to tackle an easier topic first—the Meaning of Life. I can hear you saying, "Bob, what a wuss-ass. Why not take on a challenge like world hunger or global warming?" You're being over critical. I am not about to compete with Al Gore. I'm sorry, but I'm sticking with the easy stuff.

Living is easy. You're born—you live—you die. Nothing to it, really. Same deal for each and every one of us. We're all given about 25,550 days. Time is our one and only true asset. The only thing separating one person from another is the part between the first and second dashes, the "you live" part.

There ya go. Now that we've got that settled, there's not much point in going any further and wasting what precious little time you have left reading this lame book. We've taken on the tough issues and prevailed (curtain, please). Alrighty then, it appears as though you could care less about wasting your precious time, so let's move on, shall we? Like any good mountain hike, feel free to turn around at any point along the way.

Between the "live" and "die" parts, there are people who become rich and famous and there are people who become poor and unknown. There are good guys and there are bad guys, but the bad ones are too creepy to talk about, so since it's my book, we won't mention them.

How and why does that happen? Better yet, does it matter even a little bit? Depends on whom you talk to; or listen to. Yes, there have been some great people who have done great things. Will it matter in 100 years? A thousand years? Is it possible that the lowliest person on the planet may have, in some unimaginable way, made all the difference?

Beats me. I don't pretend to have the answers. I just know what I've seen over nearly six decades. No different than anyone else who's lived this long. So, I guess from here on all I can do is share with you the very limited experiences that I've had living in one of the smallest and oddest states in the country. Chances are you've lived a more exciting life, and I can't understand why you haven't parked your butt in front of your own PC and written your own book.

There are only about 600,000 people in Vermont, the equivalent of a few city blocks in Manhattan. It's possible to go for quite some time without seeing anyone here, but it's not healthy to do that. It's sometimes tough to get a quorum, but as a rule, it's likely that you'll find enough folks to have a coffee or just a good bull session. Depending upon how long you've lived here it's almost impossible not to do the latter.

From an outsider's perspective it may not initially appear as though we do much here. Vermont finally has its own bumper sticker, "What happens in Vermont, stays in Vermont; but nothing really happens in Vermont."

At first glance, it could be hard to determine things like "what we do for work" or "what do we do for fun." What we do for fun is difficult to explain to folks unfamiliar with the Vermont way of life. Try thinking of what cavemen did. Now, think of that guy with a snowmobile or an ATV.

In 1979 I met a teenage girl from New York City. She was in the way. She was sitting on a lawn that I was trying to mow in Dorset, Vermont. I mowed lawns from the mid-1970s to the early 1980s, primarily because there was no other work in Vermont at that time (sort of like today, now that you think about it) and I had to do something. I bought a lawn mowing company from a distant relative who had a heart attack. I ended up buying two British machines known as Locke lawn mowers, a 1957 Ford pick-up truck, and 14 accounts. I was in business. Of course, I couldn't survive on 14 accounts, so with the help of my friend Jeff Hills, we designed and sent out 3,000 postcards announcing the news that I was in business!

[3]

One of the greatest fears I ever had was what would I have done if 10% of those who got that card responded, saying they wanted my service. Fortunately (I think), only about 60 replied. I was more in business than I had previously been. But I digress.

The girl had bright red hair, somewhat like my mom's hair, but no one ever had hair that red. More on Mom later. She, the teenager, looked a little bored and dejected. She didn't look like she was having a great time. Maybe it was just me, but hey, I was younger then. She could've at least smiled but didn't.

I did what any self-respecting Vermonter would do. No, I didn't run over her. I shut down the mower and said hello. She showed no overt signs of moving. I introduced myself. I don't recall if she stated her name. I doubt it. I asked, "Where you from?" "New York City" was the reply. "Big place," I said as I waited patiently for her to move so I could continue working.

She looked up at me and said, "What do you do here for fun?" That was thirty years ago, in the summer of 1979, and I'm still wondering how to answer that question. I vaguely recall looking at this person ten years my junior and a zillion miles away from the life I had been born into and realized that whatever I said was going to sound alien to her. This was the verbal encounter equivalent of Evil Knievel jumping the Grand Canyon. What could a Vermont redneck lawn-jockey tell a kid from New York City what we do here for fun? Hunt squirrels? Burn a stack of old tires? Work on your car that you know will never have a prayer of a chance of running again? Wander off into the woods for a few days? Attend a biker party of Harley Davidson fans and watch them burn a brush pile with a Japanese motorcycle on top? Swim in the local quarry? Yes, I've done all of the above. You learn to make your own fun in Vermont, but that doesn't make it any easier to explain.

If you ponder long enough, you stumble on an answer. "Go to the quarry," I said. The look on her face clearly indicated that this was

[4]

not the best answer since I doubt that New Yorkers have an abundance of quarry swimming holes or would go there if they did.

"Go to the quarry? And do what?" she asked. "Oh, uh, swim. Sorry, guess you might have thought that I was suggesting that you grab your sledge hammer and go extract some rock for another museum down there in Washington, eh?"

Yessiree, there I was bonding with a kid from New York City. OK, so maybe she looked at me like I had grown additional appendages, but I could really feel the connection. She got up and went into the house without another word. I was able to finish mowing the lawn. So you see, if you're patient, things usually work out.

Let's get back to that second dash mark up above; the one between "live" and "die." There are folks out there who don't do much more than worry about dying, which I find amusing since that pretty much is the end game for everyone. Years ago I saw a bumper sticker that read, "Welcome to planet earth. No one gets out alive." Of the three things "born—live—die," two of them are completely and totally predictable. The "born" part we, as individuals, have little control over. And the same holds true for the "die" part. Many of you are in a state of denial about the "die" part, because few of you can picture the world without you in it. What a boring place this would be without, say, me running around writing this book? It'd be like the boring place where that kid from NYC found herself on that glorious, sunny, cobalt blue sky, August day.

At the risk of sounding like Don Rumsfeld, if we know what we know, then why waste time worrying about what we know we know...or don't know. Or something like that. I never liked Rumsfeld much. We know we're born (even if we didn't know it at the time) and we know we're gonna die. So why spend one second of the short 25,550 days you have worrying about either one? You'd be better off wasting it reading this book.

[5]

It does seem as though many folks fret about things over which they have no control, and although I've not done one lick of research on the matter, I believe that the more money you've got, the more you dwell on dying. Mind you, I can't prove it; I am just going by what I've seen. People who don't seem to have all that much in terms of money don't seem to give a rat's ass about dying. They tend not to be too bored either. Starvation can take your mind off just about anything…except food, of course.

It makes sense if you think about it. Poor folks are too busy worrying about being poor. They're worrying about how they're going to get through the day, much less the whole dang life. They don't have a lick of time or resources to contemplate the end of their days, as they are somewhat preoccupied with the task of trying to put a meal on the table for their kids.

Rich folks, on the other hand, are, well, rich. More power to 'em. A long time ago I saw a book on the desk of one of my wife's coworkers titled, *The Rich Are Different.* No kidding? It should have been *We're All Different,* but I guess this book was slightly more focused. I am glad that I saw that book because up until that point in time, I wasn't completely sure if that was the case. I grew up around folks who were pretty well off—well, more well off than my family and friends and I were, anyway. I suspected that they were a little different. Seeing the title of that book served to confirm those suspicions. I have sometimes wondered had I NOT seen that book on that desk at that point in time, if I would have ever come to that conclusion on my own. Another one of life's many mysteries. I digress again. <u>Most likely there will be more on rich and poor folks later since that's all I've ever known to exist in Vermont.</u> I should note here that not all Vermonters are poor and not all newcomers to the state are rich. We have a healthy mix of each.

For now, let's get back to determining the meaning of life and talk about dying, shall we? Like I said, poor people are too busy living to worry about dying. Now, rich people, on the other hand have what? Money, duh. There are two kinds of rich people (don't

[6]

worry; generally speaking, both are just as rich). There are those who made money and those who just "have" money. It probably is irrelevant in the long run, but it's worth noting. I'm fine with either one.

With money comes various luxuries, like big houses, big cars, big boats, big planes, big wallets, big sunglasses, big-just-about-everything. Thus money = BIG. It also means that you have big time on your hands. You most likely don't have to dwell on the mundane things like starvation, because you have plenty of money and BIG food going on. So that frees up a big block of time right there. If you're very wealthy, you may have help like maids, cooks, lawn-jockeys, mechanics, plumbers, etc., who allow you to have even more time. Poor folks tend to have to do all that stuff themselves, which is why they're poor, or maybe it's vice versa. I'm not really sure.

If you're in love, being poor is much easier. In 1969 I met a young girl from Massachusetts who had the coolest name I had ever heard—Alison Vickery. We met in the registration line at Castleton State College. She was sort of involved with another guy. He had to go. We didn't miss him. We were married four years later. We were kids with less than no money, but we had each other. After classes ended we would go for long walks on the railroad tracks, trying to determine who could walk on top of the rail the farthest. Our company together was about all the wealth we needed.

During the summer of '73, I stayed in Vermont to "work and save money" while Alison went back to Mansfield, Massachusetts, to grow flowers for our wedding. I saved up about 50 bucks and she grew about three sad flowers. Neither one of us could have cared less. We just wanted to be together. On our wedding day, flowers mysteriously showed up (thanks to my mother-in-law) and after all the gifts were in, we ended up with about $75.

That was a fortune for us and we did the only thing we could do— bought a stereo. I found us a place to live called "The Dog

House." This seemed more than appropriate for me. It was a bungalow with one big 19 x 19-foot room, a tiny galley kitchen, and a bedroom that almost accommodated a bed. The place was surrounded by a dark, mysterious pine forest where we would spend nearly every day exploring. We had no choice. There was not a train for miles.

Life moved on and so did we. We built our own home with just about no money. Raised two kids. Bought used cars. Got a dog. Sent the kids to college. The dog died and we got another dog. And on and on.

Looking back, it can all be summed up very simply: There is really nothing of greater worth than walking on railroad tracks holding hands with the one you love. Everything else is just white noise.

Now that we have that cleared up, let's move on, shall we? I know, I know…you're still waiting to hear how to make it through a recession. Getting through this book will be tough enough, so just keep reading and you'll be fine. I promise.

Maybe this column that appeared in the *Bennington Banner* on April 4, 2009, might help to clear this all up. It was originally titled "Trees." The editor changed it. We forgive him.

Clinging to the rocks

I do a fair amount of driving and I spend some time on I-89. I've made this trip hundreds of times over the past three decades, but last week I noticed something that I had to have seen on every trip but never registered. Trees.

Before you think that I've finally fallen into the abyss of late middle age, let me assure you that I think I'm fine (that's probably the last thing one says prior to stepping off the ledge). There are sections on the side of this interstate that consist of nothing but rock. This is true of just about every road in Vermont, but I'm talking about what I saw here on this road.

[8]

Interstate-89 was built in the 1960s, not all that long ago for some of us; a lifetime ago for others. Trees have grown up over the nearly five decades since the ground was ravaged, ledge was blasted and pavement laid down to make our journey through Vermont all that much more enjoyable and faster.

I'm not talking about the beautiful trees in the median strip or the lovely forests that soften the view left and right. I'm talking about the skinny, scrawny, desperate trees that have sprouted out of the solid rock and are clinging on for dear life. It's one of life's marvels to think how a seed can travel through the air, land in the crevice dividing stone and somehow spring to life. It goes without saying that these poor, unfortunate trees are not nearly as robust and healthy as the other trees that had the good fortune of landing in the rich soil that lies elsewhere.

It appears to matter little to the dwarfed trees that their entire life's work consists of simply hanging on for dear life as others pass them by at speed unimaginable 100 years ago. Are they angry that their fate was determined by a howling wind? Are they disappointed that they would never be like the other, bigger, more handsome trees?

The trees that I finally had noticed vanished within seconds. They remained in my rear view mirror only a moment longer. They caused me to think about people I have known from all walks of life; people who have lived a life of good fortune and people who have lived a good life with very little.

There are many who have achieved success (whatever that means) due to their social status. They had to do little more than to be born into the right family. There are others, many more, who might have been successful had they not been born into a world of poverty. Some of the fortunate ones who live in a stratum of life where the "little people" seem of little consequence may look down upon these less fortunate people. They have it all. Resources. Good upbringing. Opportunities galore. They have hope for a better

[9]

future. They may have all of this simply because they were lucky at birth.

The poor have little. They don't get to live life; they get to cling to it. They have no resources. Their upbringing may have been weak at best. Opportunities are few. Hope wanes with each passing day. But cling they must if they are to survive another day. In our country it is possible for one of few financial resources to achieve great things. It is by no means easy.

To elevate from abject poverty to financial success takes remarkable drive and determination. You have to be smart, determined and fight every step of the way. You cannot be discouraged even for one minute; say nothing about one day. You can't feel sorry for yourself because of the bad cards you were dealt. You have to achieve the impossible as you watch others speed right on by.

If you put up the best fight possible, the odds of success are probably still against you. For the more fortunate, at times it seems that they have to do nothing more than to get dressed in the morning and the day will just fall into place, for the seed responsible for their existence had the benefit of landing in good earth with nutritious soils.

It all seems so random, doesn't it? I have known fortunate people who seem to take life for granted. It doesn't make them good or bad, but it affords them an outlook that others cannot have. I have known many more folks less fortunate, for whom life is a struggle. On average they tend to be slightly more cheerful. It's hard for them to hold on yet they get by. They want what they need and need what they've got. They have managed to cling to the rocks and against all odds somehow survive.

It may be easier and more pleasant to gaze upon the majestic, healthy trees and ignore those other poor, destitute trees growing out of rocks, but it shouldn't be about being easy. Sometimes we don't see the trees, because of the forest.

Saturday, April 4

Chapter 2.

It's All About Living

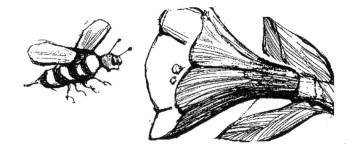

Life is about living, unless you're really rich. In the first chapter we discussed how it seems as though poor people focus more on living than rich people do. Poor people, and I generalize here, don't pay much attention to the idea of dying. Alright, they know that they are going to kick off at some point, and it may nag at them in the back of their brain somewhere, but it's not like it's the biggest deal in their average day. They are preoccupied with avoiding pesky things like starvation, creditors, things breaking that they might not know right off how to fix and then have to go to a friend or neighbor and, heaven forbid, ask for help or advice. (For those of you who are not Vermonters, the only thing worse than dying is asking someone for help. We just don't do that here.)

Generally speaking, rich folks have got that, and just about everything else, covered. So, not having to be plagued with the regular day-to-day catastrophes of living, they have the luxury of simply worrying about dying. In addition, should they fly off the road in a snowstorm, they would think nothing of asking someone to help pull them out. A Vermonter would prefer to freeze to death in a position that indicated he was attempting to push out the car by himself. That would at least make the family proud.

Better be careful of what you eat, drink, wear, what stock you buy, locking your house, where you walk, whom you meet, because making a mistake can kill you. Then what? Then you're dead. Once you're dead, as they say, you can't take it with you, which implies that not only are you dead, but you're now broke, too. Perhaps the only thing more terrifying than dying for a rich person would be facing the reality of being broke for all eternity. Being dead and broke is too hard for rich people to even get their heads around. As of right now, thanks to this nasty recession, many people in this category are now broke and still alive. That ain't good.

For the idle rich, death becomes the driving factor of day-to-day living. Don't step off that curb or you might be hit by a car and then you'd be dead...and broke, because ya can't take it with you. That's why you see poor folks wandering right across the road

[13]

without a care in the world. For that matter, poor people will take all kinds of risks, like going into strange bars, eating junk food, driving willy-nilly down the road in a snowstorm without a care in the world, sleeping on a sidewalk or, in inclement weather, in a culvert. They'll drink beer while eating Cheese-wiz and riding snowmobiles.

The non-rich guy is busy praying that the motor mounts he replaced by himself a week ago will remain in place as he's cruising down the highway at 80 mph, so he doesn't have to face the prospects of watching the motor fly through the windshield. The concern would not be impending death from a 500-pound motor crashing into his face. No, it's not the fear of dying that concerns this driver, so much as it is the idea of knowing that his friends and relatives would remember him for all time as the dork who neglected to fully tighten down the motor mounts. Now that's something to worry about.

Many poor people could care less if they check out. What the hell; wherever we're going can't possibly be worse than being here, can it? Islamic terrorists imagine being flocked by 70 virgins. Poor Vermonters envision a place that has a continuously full woodbin or a roof that doesn't leak.

Rich people, (including some Vermonters too) on the other hand, are rich. They've got it all. Go where they want, do what they want. No worries except for the one.

Watch out for that (fill in the blank) because it might kill us and then what? No more trips to Paris or caviar or wicked-nice cars. You see, death for the rich brings all of the good things to an end. Death for poor folks brings all the bad things to an end. They both reach the same end, but they are not likely to see it the same way. Makes you wonder if maybe being rich isn't all it's cracked up to be. To quote David Henry Sterry, "One unexpected benefit of the worst economic depression in a century is that for the first time in history, poor people are happier than rich people. Experts claim this is because the lifestyle of poor people has barely changed with

[14]

the economic downturn. They were below the poverty level before, and they're below the poverty level now." Bingo!

There you have it. Being rich, in the end, leaves you with nothing more than great anxiety about being poor. Being poor, in the end, leaves you exhilarated at the prospects of going to a better place; a place where you know for certain the motor mounts are properly tightened down. Now, I know what you're saying. You're saying, "Jeez, Bob, you're really full of beans here," but guess what— there are a boatload more poor people in the world than there are rich people. Just do the math and bet on the horse most favored to win. Throw your money in your favorite swimming hole (or just send it to me). Shed that horrible burden and get on with being poor and learning how to really live. You see, it's not dying that's the problem; it's fear that's the problem.

Listening to Bees

It's Sunday morning and although it's been light enough to see for over an hour the sky is grey. There is a fine mist in the air and you just know it's going to rain. The only question is when and how hard. It might just be the best time of day on the best day of the week.

I'm still in my pajamas wearing my red bathrobe and high, black, rubber pack boots and a baseball hat. I'm hoping my neighbors are sleeping in. I know my wife, Alison, is. To a stranger I thought I must look some old man who has escaped from the nursing home, but I didn't much care.

With the protection of my giant boots (with the pajamas carelessly stuffed inside) I walked into my freshly tilled garden. It was like walking on soft cotton. I sunk down a good two to three inches with every step. There is an area that I don't till, which houses four blueberry bushes planted just last year. The handful blueberries that the plants yielded where eaten by birds. Presumably they were grateful.

[15]

This year the bushes have dozens of blossoms and it's very apparent that I must get netting over them right away. Either that or I will have more bird friends than necessary. The falling mist has now covered my glasses just enough so that I feel as though I am experiencing the affects of glaucoma. I remove them and put them in the right pocket of my robe. They're done for until I get back inside.

The blueberry bushes are separated from the main portion of our garden by a large, stone walkway. On the garden side of the walkway is rich, dark brown dirt. On the other is a soft bed of pine needles that I will continue adding to over the coming years. Blueberries are acid lovers and since I'm surrounded by white pine trees, it makes for a lovely, organic ground cover.

But of course, there are weeds. Yes, already the weeds are making their traditional appearance and now is the time to get busy. They'll be tough to get out in a month or so. I scrape the dirt off the rocks; some of which are nearly completely buried. These are pretty good size rocks that were carefully removed from the stonewall that surrounds my property. Removing rocks from stonewalls in Vermont should be a crime; unless of course you are putting them an even better use. I struggled over this decision for some time. Looking at the pathway I think I made the right decision. If not, I can always lug them back from whence they came.

I am pulling weeds as the misting rain is landing on the back of my neck. The air smells great. The blueberry bush on my immediate left is playing host to my first bumble bee of the season. This black and yellow ball of wings and fiber sits comfortable on a tiny branch as he (or she; I don't know about you, but I sure can't tell the difference) extracts the pollen from newly opened leaves. He is guaranteeing a right handsome crop of blueberries in a couple of months. The bee leaves one branch to go to another; and another. The deep, throaty sound is unlike that of any bee. Bumblebees are like the Harley Davidsons of bees. I find myself listening very carefully to the sound this big fella is making and I can't help but

[16]

think how wonderful my luck is that I have "music" to pull weeds by.

I ask myself if this bumblebee is as aware of me as I am of him. I know for sure that I'm not making nearly as much noise, but on the other hand I must look like the Empire State Building to him. He looks like he could care less. Here is this creature the size of a big marble tending to his business as this creature the relative size of a 120 story building gawks and stares. Yet it is people who tend to be afraid of the bee. When the bumblebee inadvertently veers off course and "buzzes" us; we jump. Some of us shriek. Some of us try to kill the bee in spite of the fact that bee means us no harm. He's only curious to find out if we have any pollen to share.

It is our fear that causes us humans to react, sometimes violently, to those who mean us no harm. I ponder on how different our lives would be if we could learn to show no fear. Would we ever have conflict? Would we go to war? Perhaps we would all just get along. One hardly ever sees bumblebees fighting over pollen. You can learn a lot in your garden on a drizzly Sunday morning.

June 17, 2005

Chapter 3

A Flatlander's Guide for Living in Vermont (or anywhere else) During the Next Great Recession (which is all the time in Vermont)

Now that we have resolved the issue of the meaning of life we can now move on to other, more important things, such as what makes up a Vermont life or who cares, really?

The second question is easily answered. YOU. Since you bought this book we could conclude that it is YOU who cares about what goes into making a life in Vermont (oh, and how to survive a recession; can't forget about that). You're sitting there wondering what it is that makes those people in that quirky little state tick. We wish you the best of luck finding the answer. Let us know when you do. We'll review your conclusions and then tell you you're wrong. Don't give up, though. It adds to the fun of being a Vermonter.

People think that living in Vermont is a cakewalk. Limited life experience has shown me that living is easier just about anywhere else. That's why people leave here right after Christmas and come back after Memorial Day. That is probably why I've stayed here. I've convinced myself that an easy life is probably not one worth living.

At the risk of starting yet another Revolutionary War, I would offer the following bold statement: Vermont is the original Flatlander state. Vermonters like to refer to anyone not from Vermont as a Flatlander. It's just a word to let all of those who do not have "family in the ground," as we like to say, know that they are not from here. Outside of that, it doesn't really mean squat anymore. Vermont has pretty much been overrun by new Flatlanders, much like two hundred years ago when it was overrun by old Flatlanders.

Most Vermonters don't find it at all odd that one of their original heroes, Ethan Allen, was from Litchfield, Connecticut. Leave it to a state that consists of a people whose ancestors came from Litchfield, Connecticut, to look down their noses at people from, say, Litchfield, Connecticut.
But once you get to know us, all those prejudices and preconceived notions disappear like the setting sun over one of our majestic mountains. That is, until the new "Flatlander" does something

remarkably lame; something that would make any self-respecting Vermonter crawl into the basement and break out a bottle of hard cider they were saving for a special occasion.

Let me offer an example. I built my own house in 1979. It was a recessionary time, but then again, aren't they all? I bought a piece of land from a friend of my father about a month after my father had the good sense to move on. (More on the land purchase later.) I had a crew of great guys, including Carl Bucholt, who lives next door to me to this day, help me with the post-and-beam frame, windows, doors, roof, siding, etc. My employee in my lawn business, Gordon King, and I finished off the interior, which of course is why it doesn't look anything at all like the outside of the house. Suffice it to say that I was not an expert carpenter at the time, but I did get the job done (unless you choose to bring up the errant closets that have yet to be completed. We're workin' on it).

The new driveway, consisting of bank-run gravel placed over giant rocks, had recently been installed. The new driveway was pretty soft around the edges where cars and trucks had not yet packed it down. I was trimming out a window in what was to be my daughter, Meredith's, new bedroom, when I heard a car pull in. I wasn't expecting anybody but wasn't particularly alarmed. (Vermonters don't get too jazzed up when someone accidentally drives a quarter mile out of their way only to end up at someone's house on a dead end, terrified that they will be shot—or worse, asked what they're doing here. As a rule they feel compelled to flee.)

I kept hammering away, assuming that the station wagon with New Jersey plates would gracefully turn around and, like a cat that falls off the table and begins to lick itself as though nothing happened, slowly head back from whence it came.

I tend not to be that lucky. I couldn't hammer loud enough to drown out the sound of spinning tires. I peaked around the window and watched as the spinning tires were rapidly destroying the new driveway. Then there was this amazing visual.

Here was a family of four: Mom, Dad, and two little kids, all of them outside the car. The car was IN GEAR and Mom and Dad and the kids were behind it, trying to push it out of the soft, perimeter gravel where it now was very stuck, and getting more stuck by the minute.

This was not a good thing, from my point of view, because the only thing worse than having this family from New Jersey stuck in my driveway was having them standing in my driveway as their car, passenger-less and driver-less, went cruising down my long driveway and crashing into lord knows what.

I unhooked my carpenter's pouch (just wearing one of those things make you feel you are a carpenter) and went downstairs. I hadn't noticed the shirt I was wearing. It was a T-shirt with the Superman "S" emblem on it. My sister-in-law, Meredith, had given me this shirt for my birthday a year ago. We assumed the "S" was for Stannard.

"OH MY GOD!" the Mom said. "Look—it's Superman!" I looked straight up in the air. Didn't see a thing. "You stuck?" I asked. Dad looked very humble. I think he assumed that he was about to meet the end of his days. What he didn't know is that any, make that ALL, Vermonters would have no desire to kill him. We would much prefer that he live so that we can talk about him at the coffee shop for the rest of our lives, and his.

"What was your plan had you been successful in pushing the car out?" I asked. Perplexed, Mom and Dad looked at each other. The kids were still staring, wide-eyed, at the "S" on my shirt, probably wondering why I wasn't flying around.

"Guess I would have run and jumped in the driver's seat," said Dad. It was fortunate that I came along, as the Dad was running the risk of being the 1979 recipient of the famous "Darwin Awards." We got Mom behind the wheel, and Dad and I and the kids all heave-hoed and out popped the car. They ended up building a house just up the road. The daughter grew up to be our babysitter. Real close by. It all worked out. It usually does.

Life's little mishaps happen all the time.

"That Should Be Easy"

"Oh yeah, that'll be easy." How many times have you said this? You have a little drip, drip, drip under your kitchen sink. You think, "well, all I have to do is to tighten that little nut up there and I'm golden." You get what you think are the right tools; well OK, maybe not really the right tools but you know your stuff. You know that even without the right tools that you can tackle this problem.

You clean out all of the items that you keep under your sink, get your flashlight balanced precariously so that its beam illuminates the leaking fixture in question. You grab your tools and try one after another to see if it will do the job. One almost does the trick, but it slips off the nut and now the drip turns into a drizzle. Darn.

You reach for another wrench and attempt to tighten the nut again, but now something, you're not really sure just what, happens. The precariously balanced flashlight has now tipped over and you have water streaming from what was only a moment ago a drip. Now what? Call for help? That would involve sacrificing your ego. Can't do that. Things are not going well. Your friend shows up and asks, "What are you doing?" You realize that you may not have an answer to that question.

Tomorrow, Monday, March 19, marks the four-year anniversary of the United States' attack on the country of Iraq. We were convinced by our president that all options had been explored and come to an end. Iraq had weapons of mass destruction and it was well on its way towards developing nuclear capabilities. Iraq had ties to those who attacked our nation and it was, beyond any doubt, a threat to our national security.

We were led to believe that the war we were about to start would be swift and complete. "Shock and Awe" was how it was described. Our vice president told us we would be welcome as liberators and Iraqis would toss flowers and chocolate at the troops.

Four years later we now learn that none of this was true. Iraq turned out not to be the threat we were led to believe, and today Iraq is embroiled in a civil war. The task that a senior military planner told *The Daily News* on March 12, 2003: "an attack on Iraq could last as few as seven days" has proven to be wrong by three years and fifty-one weeks.

Our leadership has been wrong on almost every prediction and scenario that they presented to the American people. Americans want to believe in and trust their leaders to do the right thing and to be honest with them. Leaders pay a price when they don't tell the truth. Former President Bill Clinton knows this to be true.

It seems inevitable that a price will be paid by someone sometime soon for the mistakes, misdeeds and untruths that substantiated the need to go to war with Iraq. The retribution may not be laid at the feet of those responsible, but instead on those who will remain after those responsible have left office. That's unfortunate, but it may be the reality.

There is much more to the tale of why we had to go to war. The vice president's chief of staff has just been convicted of lying to a Grand Jury. It is clear that he is a scapegoat and a cloud of suspicion now exists over his old boss. The CIA agent whose cover was blown is now testifying before Congress. Members of Congress are finally looking into the issues with an intensity that we have not seen since the war's inception.

If someone, anyone, had the moxie to stand up and challenge the accusations and the "facts" that were presented and if/when the evidence didn't hold up, demand that the brakes be applied to the momentum to go to war, perhaps things would be different today.

We can all appreciate how difficult this would have been, politically, inasmuch as Congress and the White House was controlled by party. Questioning whether or not this was the right decision and if the right tools were being used before it all started would have been the right, if not the hard thing to do. It's a mistake that we can all learn from.

Not unlike fixing a leaking sink.

March 18, 2007

Chapter 4.

Buying Land in a Recession

OK, so the economy is in the crapper or terrorists have struck your hometown or you're just plain sick of it all and you want to move to Vermont. Have you considered another state? If not, please do. Nothing personal, mind you, but there are plenty of us here already and although there's tons of room for zillions more people, we would prefer that you go to Florida where we both know that you'll be much happier. Did I mention that it gets really freakin' cold here? The natives are some nasty characters, too. Oh, and bears. We have bears. Big mean, nasty, smelly bears with really big teeth. Coyotes, too. They'll eat your cats in a New York minute. This is one dangerous place. I wouldn't come here if I were you.

I'm going out on a limb here, but I'm betting you're on your way. You will either need to buy an existing house (preferably) or carve up more land and build a new house (not preferable, but that's what I did, but I'm a native, so I get to do that. Think of it like the Flatlander thing).

Buying land in Vermont today is much different than it was in 1978. That was the year my wife, Alison, and I bought our 2.02 acres of planet earth. If you were to buy this land today, you would need the following:

A lot of money
An engineer
A lawyer
A banker
A psychiatrist
A priest (or some other spiritual guide)
A dowser would probably be a good idea
An architect
More money than you budgeted for
A builder or contractor
A boatload of money
Patience
More money
Patience

Nerves of steel
A bottle of Jack Daniels or Single Malt Scotch (a good idea in general)
A little more money

Not having any of the above (except for the bottle of J.D.), I was at slightly more of a disadvantage in '78 than you might be today. I had $2,000 and no clue about much of anything.

At the time, land was selling for, best you sit down here, $3,300 per acre. Today one would need a substantial portion of the Obama Administration's Stimulus Package just for a down payment on two acres in Vermont. But that is now, this was then.

I asked my dying father if he knew of anyone that I might approach about buying land, since he knew everyone and their brother. He gave me the name of an old family friend, Everett Arnold. He said, "I think Everett's breaking up the old Wideawake Farm. You might want to talk to him."

My Dad died. I grieved. Got over it and went to see his Everett, who informed me that he, indeed, was selling off some land. "It's $3,300 bucks an acre, but I'll sell it to you for $2,200 an acre because I liked your dad," he said. "Oh, and you'll have to put in the drive from the main road to your property. You OK with that?" "Sure," I said. What the hell did I know about driveways and their costs? As previously mentioned I only had less than half of what I needed to buy the land. I asked if I could pay this off over time, as it took me all my life to save up two grand. "Sure," he said. What I didn't negotiate at that time was the terms for "paying off over time." My thoughts were paying it off over, say, a thousand years or so. His idea was six months. Best not to have confusion in a land deal.

I had a plan, sort of, kind of. My plan was to go to the bank and borrow enough money to build a house and to pay off the land. I know what you're saying, "Dang, Bob, that's a great plan." Boy, you don't know the first thing about buying land, do you?

[26]

I went to see my banker (who coincidentally was the captain of my volleyball team at the time). For good luck, I brought along a builder, Mike Morris, who agreed to build the shell of my house. The banker asks all kinds of hideous questions like, "Bob, do you actually feel qualified to build your own home?" Say what? Hell no. I had never built anything in my life. Well, when I was in sixth grade I built a wooden replica of the Monitor Civil War boat (which I proudly still have today…somewhere) but had I not told you the name, you would not have recognized it as such. I replied, "I guess as long as R.K. Miles (that was the local lumberyard) can make 18-inch-wide molding, I should be able to cover up just about any mistakes I make."

My smart-ass comment did little to assure my banker's faith in my ability to complete the task. Nonetheless, this brave banker of yore agreed to do a deal with me. We set up Robert J. Stannard Construction Co. and applied for a construction loan to build a speculation (spec) house. You could no more do this today than get a seat on the next space shuttle. Banking was more equitable back then. It's a mess today because they lost touch with their customers. Plus, they turned into greedy bastards. We allowed banks to merge on a grand scale and ruined hometown banking as we know it. We went from knowing our banker to not knowing if the bank that held our money was still in America. But I digress. Again.

A few days before the "Big Closing" on the construction loan, I'd told my banker that I was not going to be able to put any cash down on this deal (like I had any).

"What do you have for collateral?" he inquired. "Do you own anything?"

Hell, no, I thought to myself. Wait a minute. I kinda, sorta, almost owned some land. "Sure I do. I own the land that I'm building the house on." I had no doubt that at some point, perhaps long into the future, I would be forgiven for this miniscule breach of the truth. "That'll work," my banker-friend said.

The day of the closing I called to make sure everything was A-OK and my banker-friend said it was. "Oh, and don't forget to bring the deed with you." Life sure is full of little surprises sometimes. I drove out to Danby where Everett lived. I climbed the long flight of stairs up to his house and said, "Hi, I need to borrow the deed."

Through thick glasses with eyes squinted tight he said, "Bob, lawn mowers and ladders are things you borrow. Deeds are things you own." He was not going to make this easy.

"I know," I said, "but I just need it for today. I'll have it back to you by 5:00 p.m." He went and got the deed and handed it to me. "Uh, I'll need to have you sign this," I said.

"You haven't paid for it yet," he said.

"I know that," I replied, "but don't worry because you'll have it back by this afternoon."

Anxiety and suspicion were walking hand in hand as he signed the deed. I was getting very excited. As I reached for the signed deed, he grabbed my hand and held it tight to the kitchen table. With his other hand he pulled out a wooden drawer in his wooden kitchen table. From the drawer he pulled out a long barrel .44 Magnum pistol. "You don't have this deed back here by 5:00 p.m., I will find you and blow your fucking head right off." See, that's putting a real fine point on the art of negotiating, right there.

You know what they say about the best-laid plans? We're moving along smartly in our closing. I have a lawyer. The bank has a lawyer and papers are flying back and forth. We're signing stuff left and right. This is great. I'm about to get $27,000 to build my own house (I figured I needed only $25,000; the other two, plus the cash I had on hand, was to pay off the land).

[28]

Sure enough, the time came when my volleyball captain-banker-friend said to me, "So, do you have the deed to the land that you are putting up as collateral?"

By golly, I had that deed right there in my hot little hand. Pulled it right out and said, "Yessir, here you go. As you can see it's mine. It's signed right over to me, thank you very much," and I proceeded to put it right back in my pocket.

"Uh, Bob, the bank will need to keep that deed here in the vault. It's the collateral. It stays here." Hello! What had only moments ago been a positive and exciting time had suddenly turned ugly.

"You can't actually keep this deed," I said.

"What?" he said. Funny how people tend to go deaf when you say things they don't want to hear.

Speaking a little louder, I said again, "You can't have the deed, but as you can scc, I do own thc land."

"We better step outside here for a minute," my less than friendly friend-volleyball-captain-banker said. We left the room and went into the hallway. "What are you up to here?" bankerman asked. He was looking downright unfriendly by now. I told him that I have the deed right here and that it's signed over to me but that he can't have it. I have to keep it. He did not find this amusing, not cvcn a little bit. I said, "Tell you what. We can make a copy of it and you can have the copy. That'll work, won't it?"

Time slows right down to a crawl when things like this happen. You ever notice that? About twelve eternities clawed their way forward while my former friend-volleyball-captain-banker glared and said, "If you screw me on this, you are going to be in BIG TROUBLE." Well, duh. No kidding. I now had to weigh my options. Banker = BIG TROUBLE. Owner/seller with loaded .44 Magnum long barrel = head blown off. Some of life's choices are much easier than others.

[29]

"Don't you worry about a thing. This is all gonna work out just fine," I said. We wrapped up the closing using a copy of my deed, and I dashed out to my car and sped to Danby—straight to Everett's house. I spun into his parking lot and sprinted up the stairs. It was a few minutes before 5:00 p.m. I was safe. Life was good.

I walked into his place and oddly enough he hadn't moved. As a matter of fact, everything looked pretty much like it had when I left earlier in the day, with one obvious difference. There was a slew of empty long necks scattered on and around the kitchen table. The gun was right where it had been. My dad's friend looked a little glassy-eyed, but not much else had changed.

"Glad you made it. I was just thinking it might be about time to come lookin' for you." Nervously, I handed him back the signed deed. "Here you go." He looked at it. Looked at me. He could tell I was a little antsy.

"I bet there's a story behind this day" was all he said.

A few days later the paperwork all got processed and money became available. We paid off the balance owed on the land and got to work building a house. We paid the house off in June of 2008. For thirty years the bank had a copy of my deed. Didn't see any point in bringing down the original as having a copy seemed to work just fine. We aren't in the business of kickin' sleepin' dogs around here.

There was a time when things like banking and doing business in Vermont was done on your name and your word. Oh, yeah, and sometimes a .44 magnum. The mortgage loan crisis that our nation is experiencing as I write this was caused by bankers who lent money to people who couldn't afford to borrow it. But what was worse was that the bankers didn't really know their customers, or perhaps even care to know them. All they wanted to do was to

[30]

make the loan at all costs, which turned out to be a lot for the rest of us.

There was never any question that I was going to make good on this deal. Sure, I was motivated knowing that my father's best friend probably would shoot me, but Alison and I really wanted a home and to raise a family. The bank wanted to make a good loan. Everyone wanted to see it happen. We all worked hard to make it work. Had I failed, my late father would have never forgiven me. That's real Vermont motivation.

The entire deal was done on an 8½ x 11-inch legal pad, by the way. I would argue that the more complicated the process has become, the greater the chance that the deal fails. There's a lot to be said for knowing your friends and neighbors. It makes doing business much safer in the long run, even if it doesn't always feel like it at the time.

We've stayed on Wideawake Road for over thirty years and walked the roads and woods. I know I'll never really be able to thank Everett and Janice enough for helping to start us off.

Yesterday's Walls

I've been walking around this area in which I live for 25 years. After a lifetime I've come to realize that we take our surroundings for granted. Stonewalls. There are stonewalls on each side of road I walk. Miles of stonewalls.

This morning I spent some time reflecting on the people who built these walls and the circumstances that caused these monuments to the past to be a relevant part of our landscape today.

My ancestors would find hundreds of rocks in the fields that they needed to work to survive. They manually moved these rocks off to the side. They came to understand that these stones could serve two purposes: keeping their animals from roaming off and defining the borders of their property.

How successful were the results of their hard labor? Not very. Today, their work is barely visible through the undergrowth. Fields that took an enormous effort from grandfathers, sons and grandsons to clear are now forested. The only purpose the walls serve today is one of aesthetics.

The walls of today are built to keep people in or out, not animals. A wall was built to separate East Germans from West Germans. It worked for a while, but it was only a matter of time before it failed. The front-page debate today is how to deal with illegal immigrants coming into America. Some say we should build a wall. Yes, let's build a wall. That will keep them out.

Walls need not be built of rock and mortar. They can be constructed in one's mind. Each and every one of us is guilty of self-created barriers in one form or another. Fear is the concrete used to build these walls. Some Vermonters fear going to New York City. Some New Yorkers fear entering the woods of Vermont.
We are at war (again) with people whom we know little about and who know little about us. We have different religious beliefs. We struggle to build walls to keep them away from us. They are busy constructing walls to keep us away from them. The walls of fear now use weapons, big and small, to keep us apart.

Walls of intolerance of the beliefs of others have been responsible for wars throughout our time on the planet. It's amazing that after hundreds of years of living together (or perhaps I should say, living apart) we have not yet been able to overcome our fears stemming from religion. The "War on Terrorism" is nothing more than another religious war. Is there not some similarity between Islamic extremists and the Puritans who burned innocent women at the stake? Too much blood has saturated this planet in the name of religion. Too many walls have been built to keep us apart.

[32]

Vermonters of 150 years ago knew the value of good relationships with their neighbors. They knew that they couldn't survive on their own. Walls were built because the stones were impeding their ability to grow crops. They were low, shallow walls just high enough to keep their sheep and cows in, but low enough so that their neighbors could scale them with ease. They defined the boundaries but did little to keep people apart.

I'm not so naïve as to think that all of those who once lived here did so in complete harmony. We've always had our differences. What's changed is our level of tolerance. We are working to build bigger, thicker and more permanent walls designed to exacerbate our intolerance.

We need to spend a little more time thinking about who we are and why we're all here, because those in power today are doing little to make this world a better place. It's only a matter of time before the trees and brush grow up and their new walls become obsolete. I wonder if these new walls will be as aesthetically pleasing as the walls of yesterday.

May 7, 2006

Chapter 5.

Here's to Your Health

Health care is one of the prime reasons why we are in the fiscal situation we're in today. Gotta have it. Can't afford it.

I've never been a big fan of doctors or the drugs that they prescribe. As individuals, many of them are just fine, but as a species, doctors make me a little nervous. First of all, they know too much about medicine for my liking. Second, they don't really know much about me, or my body, or my health. The only one who really knows that stuff is me and I'm not overly excited about sharing that knowledge with anyone, especially a doctor.

That doesn't mean I don't like them, per se. They're fun to be with at cocktail parties and stuff, but just don't wear that stethoscope around your neck while your chattin' away about doing a colonoscopy or something. Jeez. Do we need that?

Doctors are forgivable. Drug companies. That's a different story. They should all be gracefully let out to pasture. Make that the upper pastures. Maybe it's because I had a not-so-funny doctor story early in life is why I still harbor these ill feelings toward the medical profession. Think of it as how your dog must feel about the invention of the invisible fence.

Norbert , Charlie, and Siggy made up the Buchmayr triplets for whom my grandmother, Thyra Erk, had been a nanny. That's how she got the name of "Nanny." Siggy is the sole surviving triplet today. That he is still with us is incredible. It was a miracle that any of them lived through their teens. They were some of the wildest people I have ever known and are still legends in this part of the state. I had many adventures with these three guys who were eleven years my senior, but always treated me as an equal. Generally when we got together we had a pretty good time. The day in the summer of 1968 when Norbert, Charlie, and I were stacking wood was not one of those times.

Norbert was in a pickup truck half full of firewood. Charlie was in the basement stacking as Norbert tossed logs off the truck. Norbert would throw the wood from the truck toward the small, basement

[35]

window and then jump off the truck, go over to the pile by the window, and pitch the wood into the basement, nearly killing Charlie in the process. On any given day, Charlie was generally eligible to be killed by either brother for almost any reason in the unlikely event they felt they needed one.

My arrival in my 1963 Ford Falcon convertible could not have been timelier. "Sit over there by the basement window, Bobby (they all called me "Bobby" because in my younger days I looked very much like Howdy Doody. "Bobby" was more acceptable than Howdy). I'll toss the wood to you and you toss it to Charlie."

The best laid plans. About ten pieces of wood into this project, Norbert tossed a piece that had a pretty big bulge on one end. Now, you need to understand one thing here. It only took tossing one piece of wood for the three of us to develop a pretty darn good system. A log would come flying at me from Norbert who was about 15 feet away. It would hit the ground. I would grab it and stuff it through the window. Charlie would snag it and stack it immediately. Slicker than dog doo.

Until the bulgy piece, that is. I could tell as it was in the air that it was going to be a problem. It hit the ground. I grabbed it and tried to stuff it in the small, rectangular window. Wouldn't fit that way. I pulled it out and turned it a quarter turn. I firmly gripped it with both hands and pulled it back for a second shot at the window.

When a near perfect chain like the one we had going on is broken, the results are never good. I paid no attention to the fact that my right thumb was on the butt end of this log, facing Norbert who had already launched the next piece of wood.
Norbert Buchmayr was world renowned for his skeet shooting abilities. He was one hell of a good shot. He wasn't bad with a piece of firewood either. His oncoming log hit squarely on the end of the bulgy log that I was drawing back for a second attempt at the window.

What a really bad place for my thumb to be, crushed between two logs going in different directions. Prior to the shock of pain reaching my brain, I had looked over my shoulder to see the log that left Norbert's hand now in midair. In what developed into a slow- motion movie, I watched as log A hit perfectly onto log B. A bright crimson stream of what I later realized was my own blood shot straight out of the end of my thumb that served as a buffer between the two logs. Wouldn't want to hurt the logs.

What an interesting movie. "Man, that's gonna hurrrrrrrrrrrrrrrttttttttt." At that moment the synapse or neurons or whatever the hell they are traveled at warp speed to my brain. I didn't faint or puke, but would have had I had time to think about it. I couldn't think thanks to the searing pain blasting full speed into my head. I seem to recall that I did scream.

Norbert jumped off the truck. Charlie hollered from the basement," Where's the wood?" The scream didn't seem to impact Charlie much. I looked at what I thought could be, might be, my thumb. It was flat. I'm not talking thin here. I mean it was flat as in real flat. I was so mystified at seeing my thumb completely and thoroughly flattened that I had momentarily forgotten the fact that my brain was on fire with pain. Fortunately, that feeling came stampeding right on back and distracted me from staring at my very flat thumb.

"Wow, that must hurt!" Norbert said. He was a real comfort that Norbert. "Let's get you inside." Getting me anywhere but where I was seemed fine to me. With my hand and thumb twitching with pain, we went into their tiny kitchen in what is one of the oldest houses in Manchester, Vermont. It was a wonderful house with a tiny, galley kitchen, a homey dining area, a comfy living room. It had lots of old, dark wood. But right then I didn't care much about the house. Norbert reached behind the bar and pulled out a pint of Blackberry Brandy. This was "real doctorin' " in 1968. "Drink some of this and hold this ice on your thumb," he said. He was only lacking the stethoscope. You ever notice how ice feels more like fire when it's on a crushed thumb? Try it sometime. It's really something.

I was proud of Norbert for thinking I was able and qualified to do two things at once. I wasn't, of course, so I focused on doing just the one thing, polishing off the pint of Blackberry Brandy. Now, there's nothing in the Journal of the American Medical Association that says Blackberry Brandy will cure anything, which proves that this publication has value, because that brandy didn't do anything for me. It did, however, do something TO me.

It wasn't long before I was on my knees in front of their toilet recycling the brandy. I was feeling no pain notwithstanding my thumb, which was pounding like the bass drum in a marching band.

"I guess I better head home," I said. "I don't think I can stack much more wood." All were in agreement that I was about done stacking for the day. I'd been driving longer than was legally allowed and had some experience driving handicapped. I made it home driving with my left hand. Naturally the Ford Falcon convertible was a 4-speed stick shift, thus allowing me to relive the thumb-crushing incident every time I shifted. I believe I remained in second gear for the four-mile drive home. When you're 16 and you polish off a pint of Blackberry Brandy and you have a flattened thumb, you learn to be pretty frugal with the gas peddle. There are times when it's a good idea to drive very slowly. This was one of those times.

You'd think that this would be about enough for a good story, but too bad for you. I woke the next morning to what I thought could be ten thousand Sumo wrestlers simultaneously stomping on my thumb. The good news was that my thumb was no longer flat. The bad news was that it was about the size of a plum and the most beautiful shade of purple I had ever seen. It was a much prettier color than a plum. The nail of my thumb looked almost like there must've been a mini black light inside there. I exhaled my breath in awe of the color. The air from my mouth lightly touched my thumb. I'm pretty sure I screamed again.

My mom took one look at the thumb and said, "Bobby (yes, she, too, called me Bobby), I think you need to go to the doctor." Thinking to myself, "Couldn't we just cut the thumb off with a butter knife? How 'bout another pint of Brandy and I'll just puke a little more and it'll be fine." There are some things like your opinions on doctorin' that are best not shared with your mom. They won't influence her in the least and it'll be another argument that you will lose.

Mom took me in to see our country doctor, Cliff Harwood. Years later he and I would serve together in the Vermont Legislature. Our colleagues were shocked to learn that he had delivered me into this world. Some never forgave him for that.

"Hurt your thumb?" As a highly trained, medical physician he could diagnose a problem right off.

"Yessir," I replied; my voice, and just about everything else, trembling. I continued, "Let's try real hard not to hurt it some more."

"We're going to have to relieve the pressure," he declared. I did not like the sound of that. First off, there was no relief valve on the thumb, so I ruled out "easy" right off the bat.

"How are 'WE' going to do that, Doc?" I queried.

"I want you to grip the table right here, with your fingers under the table and your thumb on top right here." It's times like these that it would be advisable for everyone to carry a firearm. For two reasons. One, to kill yourself. Two, to kill the man who was about to "relieve the pressure." I had no firearm. I did what I was told.

Good ol' Doc now held a scalpel in his right hand. You know, one of those little things that look like an Exact-O knife. Very sharp

[39]

and angular and comes to a real sharp point. I should mention right here that at this point I did not have a good feeling about the immediate future. "I'm going to just poke a hole in the base of your thumbnail and relieve the pressure."

Say what? I looked up at my mom, hoping that she was going to say, "OK, we're outta here." Instead, she had that "Now Bobby, be stoic" look on her face. Me with no gun.

Doc is about to begin grinding away on my thumbnail when he looked up at my mom and said, "Who do you think is going to win the election?" Doc Harwood was a conservative Republican and a big Richard Nixon supporter. The scalpel touched my thumbnail. I immediately relived the moment when the two logs came together with my thumb between them, ensuring that the logs would not be damaged.

He began to twist left, then right, then left again. Not once did he look at my thumb, but instead he was chatting away with my mom about whether or not Nixon was going to do it this time. You would have thought that he would have been amused to witness my eyes bulging out of my head, but no. Political discussion always took precedent with Doc.

I never really needed any additional reasons to dislike Nixon. However, if Nixon had been Mother-freakin'-Theresa, I'm sure I would have ended up hating him for the rest of my days after that. As Doc chatted away, the tip of the razor-sharp scalpel finally broke through my black-light purple nail. You would think that this would be a great time to stop, now wouldn't you? But no. Doc was really, really interested in my mom's take on the election and he kept right on grinding. Right about here we were on the cusp of Webster's twelfth definition of "PAIN." I couldn't speak. I was frozen in place with pain. I don't believe I ever experienced anything as painful as I did that lovely fall day in his dark, dingy office.

My left hand came up out of nowhere and with a mind of its own quickly and firmly grabbed Doc by the throat. Had my brain not been quite so clouded up with pain, I'm sure it would have asked itself, "What the hell are you doing, Bob, grabbing Doc Harwood by the throat," but this was no time for silly questions.

Blood was blowing out of my thumbnail and running down the side of the table. "Well, it looks as though we got through the nail and relieved the pressure," Doc said, somewhat muffled, as I had a pretty good grip on his windpipe. He always could diagnose a problem.

Much like I have suggested that it's a good idea to be conservative with your money during these hard economic times, it doesn't hurt to be slightly more conservative when grinding a scalpel into one's over-inflated thumbnail.

It should come as no surprise a dozen years later that Doc wasn't real wild about me running for office. He could tell that I didn't like Nixon. At least he knew I had a good grip...with my left hand anyway. Things have changed in the pharmaceutical industry since the days of getting my thumb "relieved of pressure" but not all that much.

Take Two and Call Me in the Morning

I'm a pretty happy guy. I'm not rich, but I'm OK with what I have. I have a wonderful wife, two great kids and my dog seems to think I'm pretty great. Well, she acts like she does, anyway.

Now that 2005 is in our rearview mirror and we're cruising into 2006; a brand-new year. Time for resolutions, changes, a new focus on life, maybe even lose a few pounds. After New Year's we're all pretty gung-ho, aren't we? The days are now getting longer and believe it or not we're on our way towards tulips, crocuses, tilling and planting. Hope springs eternal, and the coming of a New Year is always hopeful.

[41]

I pause to think of what's bothering me. As of this writing it's a pretty short list – health care. First and foremost, I am not an expert on health care. I know what you know; it's too darned expensive. Costs are rising faster than corn in July after a heavy rain (or faster than my kids have grown; take your pick). Our elected leaders talk a lot about curbing health care costs and when they are done the costs go up again.

You may have heard the phrase, "If you think it's hard staying healthy, try getting sick." My wife and I spend a fair amount of our leisure time at our local gym doing an aerobics class known as Kabox. We jump, punch, kick, do pushups, crunches, etc. for about an hour three times per week. I practice Karate as often as I possibly can; about 1-4 times per week. My daughter does Yoga and since she now lives in Brooklyn, walks more than most deer hunters in November. We work hard to not use our medical insurance and thus far, knock on wood, that's worked pretty well.

But here's one thing that needs fixing. Congress needs to curb the pharmaceutical company's ability to advertise on television. It is pointless and it's costing someone, probably you and me, a fortune. What good does it do anyone to watch a 60 second spot that tries to convince you to take medication for something that we don't even know if have it or not? Some of these commercials are so vague that the message is simply, "go see your doctor and ask him about _____ (fill in the blank)."

If successful these senseless commercials result in having an army of mindless people traipsing in to see their doctors to ask about some drug that they know nothing about. If the multi-million (maybe even billion) dollar campaign is effective, then it is placing a needless burden on our doctors, while simultaneously adding to the cost of health care and prescription drugs.

I could be way off base on this one. Maybe it's good public policy for a company to spend a ton of money convincing us that we're sick and that we need to rush straight to our doctor and ask about "Xantracionocate" or some other incoherent medication that may cause harm to your liver, your heart, your brain, but don't worry, it'll take care of the illness that you may not have. If you do respond to these ads don't complain about your premiums. Be well in '06.

January 1, 2006

Chapter 6

Politics

I begin this section on politics by saying that there is not a more fun group of folks than those who serve the people of Vermont. It takes a certain kind of character to want to do the job to say nothing about actually getting elected. Politicians get a bad rap. They are gregarious, charming, funny, witty, and smart. I know, you're thinking that they are mostly scumbags and crooks. Not so in a small state where everyone knows their Representative and Senator and no one is bashful about bashing them face to face at the local grocery store.

Vermont has a citizen legislature, which means that they're only in session a few months of the year. The rest of the time they have to find something to do to support themselves. It is not an easy gig. It's tough on families, on careers, and on the individual. This state is fortunate that anyone ever runs for office; nevertheless, really good folks do run, year in and year out.

In late winter of 1982 a friend of mine, Seth Bongartz, called and asked me if I would be interested in running for the Vermont House of Representatives. You could've knocked me over with a mosquito fart. "Don't you have to be a lawyer to do that?" I asked.

"No, actually, it's best if you're not," he replied. (Seth became a lawyer AFTER he served. He now serves as the director of Robert Todd Lincoln's family home, known as Hildene. He's done wonders with the place). I was mowing lawns at the time and most definitely not a lawyer. Seth suggested that I go talk to a few key people in the district, including Doc Harwood, as he was the Town Republican Chairman.

"Uh, you want me to run with you as a Republican?" I asked. That was a little tough to get my head around, inasmuch as I had been a hippie for the previous decade and a half and didn't really see myself as a Republican.

"It's a Republican district and if you want to win, you have to run as a Republican. Once you get elected, the party is not that relevant in the State House." Well, well. I knew that if my dad

[45]

was still alive that he'd be amused. I come from a long line of Republicans. Actually, if your family's from Vermont, you're automatically a Republican at birth. Democrats played no role in Vermont until Phil Hoff was elected.

Phil Hoff served as Governor of Vermont from 1963 to 1969. At the time of his election, he was the first Democrat elected Governor of Vermont in 110 years. Most people thought Hoff was an anomaly. Little did they know that the Democrats would preside over the implementation of unprecedented environmental, development, and social welfare programs. Hoff ran unsuccessfully for U.S. Senate, but came back to serve with distinction in the Vermont State Senate. I was in the House when he arrived in the Senate. Phil is a pretty easy-going man and easy to befriend.

"Do I call you 'Governor' or 'Senator?' " I asked when he arrived in the State. "Both," he said with his trademark grin. To this day I call him "Governor Senator."
The thought of going to see Doc Harwood caused my body temperature to drop four or five degrees. I had seen him only once since his masterful doctoring on my thumb and that was to get a blood test for a marriage license.

It was hard for me to figure which of the memories he had of me that he might hold in the highest affection: grabbing him by the throat or showing up in coveralls with hair below my shoulders, wanting a blood test so I could get married. As a promoter of the John Birch Society, Doc never was much of a fan of the hippie movement. Alison and I were married in 1973, so it had been a while since Doc and I had chummed around together.

This day my hair was a little shorter (and thinner) as I sat in his office asking for his blessing for me to run for one of two House seats. He had that look on his face like he'd rather ingest one of the lethal drugs in the black bag that he carried everywhere he went, than to give me his OK.

[46]

"There's no question that you have name recognition and would probably win," he said forlornly. "I have a few other people I was going to approach about this," he added. Not one to take "No" for an answer, I asked, "Who?" Reluctantly he gave me the name of Ralph Fleming, who owned and operated Fleming's Hardware. "Be right back," I said as I hopped in the car to go see Ralph. Ralph Fleming was a wonderful guy. Every kid in Manchester went to his store to get fishing tackle, hunting stuff, and pretty much whatever you needed in the way of sporting goods or supplies for around the house. He was put out of business by a chain hardware store, and factory outlets now occupy the space that was once his. His store will always be remembered by the locals for the floorboards that creaked when you walked in. They, too, have been replaced.

Ralph was puffing on his pipe when I asked him if he was going to run. "Oh, hell no. I'm not doing that. Why do you ask?" he said.

I replied, "I was thinking I might run, but not if you were going to. I wouldn't stand a chance against you."

(Puff, puff.) "Nope, I'm not interested. You have at it. I think you'd do a great job." Glad he thought so, cause I had no clue.

I raced back to Doc's office and relayed the news. He sat and glared at me. His hand twitched a little like he might be going for the scalpel again. "Anyone else I should go see?" I asked and that was the end of that. Next thing you know, I was running around with a clipboard and petitions, looking for signatures so I could have my name placed on a ballot. What was I thinking?

On the campaign trail I ran into Charlie Buchmayr and told him what I was doing. "That's great, Bob. Of course, you will lose your first time out, but keep trying until you win." Always one to be supportive, Charlie was. You would've thought with the thumb episode that he might have shown a little more compassion. I think that it was his way of motivating me. There was no way I would lose this race. Charlie died last summer before I got around to telling him "thanks for the kick in the ass." That's the trouble with time. When you finally get around to saying what you want to say to your friends, they're dead. Be that a lesson to you, best not to put some things off. Say what's on your mind before your mind (or theirs) is done.

Long story short, I got elected … as a Republican. Wonders never cease. It's opening day of the legislature and I'm in the building with Alison and my mom, Thyra. We're wandering around like we have a clue what we're doing. I'm wearing a grey suit (something I found amusing after wearing cut-off jeans and T-shirts for years. I was a no-slave-to-fashion kind of guy).

We were standing in the well of the Vermont House of Representatives, admiring the very high ceilings, the chandeliers, the architecture, and the red velvet draperies. The Vermont House is a sight to behold. It's a working museum. We were caught up in the awe of the moment. The place was buzzing with the dull drone of people moving and talking.

That drone was shattered when a voice boomed, "Bob Stannard! From the SDS to the Republican Party!" I was a fringe member of SDS back in college. Seemed like the thing to do at the time. Sometimes one's past can jump right out of the bushes and bite'm right in the ass. This was one of those times.

My head retracted down into my shoulders like a frightened turtle. I didn't want to turn around, but I had to. There stood A.J. Marro; an old college buddy who was now a photographer for the *Rutland Herald*. He looked like the character Hagrid in the Harry Potter movies. "Hey, AJ," I whispered, "keep your voice down, would'ya?" "Oh, yeah, sure, no problem!" he bellowed. I think the huge chandelier in the center of the ceiling trembled slightly. The other Republicans who happened to be hanging around all looked at me like someone wearing a swastika at a bar mitzvah. A nice warm welcome to the legislature; like I dreamed it would be.

[48]

After bidding adieu to Alison and Mom, I began to reflect upon what was about to happen. I looked around the august body of the Vermont Legislature and quickly realized that I was about the only person there who was under 80. It looked like a nursing home. The Talking Heads line "you may ask yourself, how did I get here?" flew into my head. Well, it is what it is. Suck it up and make the most of it. Maybe I could help out as a nurse or something.

For the record I would say that the strangest stuff seems to happen to me. Most normal people get elected. Get sworn in. Meet new folks. Settle down and get to work. Not so for me.

Toward the end of my first day of being a legislator, I ran into Rep. Bob Graf, a Pawlet Republican. Bob had been in the legislature 22 years and sat on the all-powerful House Appropriations Committee. (Little did I know I would hold that same seat in two years.) He invited me to stop by his suite at the Tavern Motor Inn (now the Capital Plaza Hotel) across the street from the State House.

I went up to the room on the third floor. It was a larger than average motel room. It had a booth set up with benches on either side like a diner. The booth was perpendicular to the door so that when you entered the room you saw the profiles of six men, three on each side, facing each other. Against the wall on the left was a small refrigerator. There probably was a bed or two there, but to be honest, I don't recall seeing one.

I had changed out of my suit and was in jeans, flannel shirt, and leather jacket when I entered the room. I said, "Hello" and nobody spoke. The six men were intensely involved in a game of poker. In circumstances such as these, time can stretch out like taffy on a hot day. What felt like three eternities was probably only a minute or two, but damn that's a long time to be leaning up against a door casing in a room full of six guys and nobody saying a word to you. Nothing. Nada. No "hello." No "Care to join us?" Zippo.

[49]

After a geological time period had passed, without turning his head to look toward me, presumably because he dare not take his eyes off his opponents, Bob Graf said flatly, "There's beer in the fridge."

Was he talking to me? He was looking at the guy straight across from him. No one moved. No one said, "Hey there, young fella. Welcome to the legislature." Nope. I grabbed a beer, popped the top, and took a long pull. Then a second long pull. Zip. No other words spoken. The card game continued in silence. "This certainly is a great time," I thought to myself.

One thing I couldn't help noticing was the guy on the end of the left bench. Leaning on the bench behind him was a pair of crutches. His right pant leg was folded neatly into the waist of his pants. Somehow, this guy had lost his entire leg. Later, I learned his name was Leon Babbe and that he was a really good man from Swanton, Vermont. A Democrat, too, no less. Guess Seth was right about the "party thing" not being that relevant up here. Poker is a bipartisan game.

There I stood, almost done with my beer, when the door flew open and in walked Rep. Alexander "Bud" Keefe, a Democrat from Rutland City. Bud was well known to everyone. He wore a three-piece, glen plaid suit, complete with pocket silk. The Windsor knot in his tie was perfect. His hair was flowing, wavy, silver, coifed in a way that would not tolerate a single hair being out of place. He also had the most purple nose I had ever seen. It rivaled my thumb of an earlier chapter. Bud was one of the most fun guys you would ever hope to meet. An Irishman's Irishman. He was an Irish tenor who could take a man like me, not a big fan of Irish music, and bring him to tears whenever he sang those songs, most of which are way more depressing than any Blues tune I've ever heard or, for that matter, the recession in which we find ourselves. He was larger than life.

[50]

He placed his right arm around my shoulder and with his best, booming, Irish tenor voice, bellowed, "You know what the problem with the legislature is this year?" I had no way of knowing whether or not there was a problem, but I had a feeling I was about to find out. None of the poker playing lawmakers moved a muscle.

"There are too fucking many guys here with one leg." Exercising great control, I was able to not blast a mouthful of beer all over his lovely suit. The man with his pant leg stuffed into his belt didn't even flinch. I didn't know it then but another man in this poker game, Rep. Paul Robar, had lost his leg below the knee. He, too, remained motionless.

After that little fart-in-church moment had had a chance to settle down, Rep. Tom Candon, another Democrat from Rutland City, without turning his head or taking his eyes off his opponents, asked, "How's Joe?" Joe, as it turned out, was Rep. Joe Reed of Hartford. He was a large man who wore a loud, white and red plaid jacket with a plastic carnation in the lapel. I had no way of knowing that Joe and Bud were roommates and had been for many years. These guys were hardcore, legislative veterans. Joe had a severe case of the gout and was in the room adjacent to the room in which I was standing. He was quite ill.

"Joe? Joe's dead." Bud's beautiful voice resonated around the room. Wow! The problem with the legislature is that there are too many guys with one leg and some guy named Joe is dead. After about a three-second wait, there was a muffled voice that came from the paper-thin wall on my left. "I'M NOT DEAD, YOU SON-OF-A-BITCH!" Joe may have been sick, but his hearing was OK.

This was the only time I witnessed any reaction from the six men playing cards. If you watched very carefully, you could see the corners of each of their mouths move ever so slightly. "The State is in good hands," I thought to myself. I left the room.

[51]

Chapter 7

Politics—Day 2

It is very helpful to have a full understanding of the political process when trying to survive a recession. The thoughtful actions taken by a few have a pretty big impact on the lives of many. As previously stated, the Vermont General Assembly has what is known as a "citizen's legislature." I'm not exactly sure why it's called this, because I think all legislatures are made up of citizens. Vermont's a special place. We feel compelled to point out that we're citizens.

I came into my second day of work with a pretty clear understanding of how this place functioned. The poker game from the previous evening proved to be a real education. None of what I had experienced in that room was discussed in the "Freshman Orientation" that I attended in December.

I spent the second day adjusting to the fact that I was about to be working with people who knew how to deal cards and make deals. About mid-morning of the second day I met a younger representative, Leigh Tofferi, a Ludlow Democrat, with whom I would become friends and remain so until this day. Well, until he reads this book. This story is worth taking that risk, and after all, if you don't take a risk now and then, what's the point of being here? (Re-read "The Meaning of Life".) The only way to get out of a recession/depression is to take a risk now and then.

At the close of business on the second day I ran into Leigh. It was about 5:00 p.m. "Care to go to the Tavern and have a cocktail?" he asked. Little did I know the ramifications of this invite. Leigh is one of the steadiest, brightest guys I have ever met. We ended up as roommates. He's now a highly respected governmental affairs director for Blue Cross/Blue Shield of Vermont. That was now; this was then. We were slightly more rowdy then.

He and I had a lot in common, a good sense of humor, similar early life experiences, and we were about the same age. There was one primary difference. Of the two of us, Leigh could hold his liquor. It wasn't like he was in training or anything. There are people out there who have two drinks and want to take on everyone in the bar.

[54]

Then there are those who can seemingly drink forever, smile, and not show any outward signs at all that they're inebriated. Then there're guys like me, who have a few drinks and fall asleep almost immediately.

For the record I will note that Leigh no longer imbibes. He gave it up. Some guys pack it all in at once; others amortize it over a lifetime. Leigh figured life out early, which is a real credit to his strength of will power. Party hearty, then knuckle down. Too many folks never quite figure that out.

We hiked to the Tavern and plunked ourselves down in the plush, red leather chairs that occupied the space to the left of the bar.

"What are you having" he asked.

"Bourbon and water, I guess. You?"

"I'll have a scotch and water," and so began what was to become a string of adventures with this new friend. I was never a big drinker. I was about to prove that to Leigh.

We chatted away about this and that when after a few minutes Leigh asked, "Ready for another round."

"Sure. I will be by the time it arrives," I replied. I'm sipping away on my second drink when I noticed that his glass was a bit less full than mine. I have about a quarter of my drink left. " 'Bout ready for another?" he asked.

I tossed back the remainder of my second drink and said, "Sure."

I was about halfway through my third drink in about thirty minutes, when Leigh said, "Whaddya think? Ready for another round?" I should have seen what was coming. "Shhuuurrwwlll," I burbled.

Four drinks went down in just under an hour on an empty stomach. "I think I need something to eat" was my reply.

"Oh, OK, sure. We can go eat," he said agreeably.

We stood up. That seemed to be a much easier feat for him than for me. I thought I had been punched between the eyes. You could have lit a cigarette on my cheek. I hung onto the chair for good luck more than anything else. I was praying to get outside and have the cold, January air rush over me like a linebacker in a Superbowl game.

I was coming to grips with the reality that I might be able to place one foot in front of the other. We climbed the three steps that went from the bar into the lobby. I was doing great. I was going to make it to the door and everything was going to be A-OK. Ever noticed how sometimes things don't work out the way you want 'em to?

"Hey, there're some people over here I want you to meet," said Leigh. There are times in one's life when the primal instincts of early man channel through us. They shoot into the head and scream, "Run for your life" or "Don't eat that." I believe it is some sort of cosmic protective device that has allowed humans to survive as long as we have. It's unfortunate when we don't pay attention to them.

"Uh, Leigh, I'm not so sure I should really meet anyone right now," I said with a touch of worry in my voice.

"Come on. You're fine. These guys are great," he said. All this scene was missing was the music in an Alfred Hitchcock movie when the poor, unsuspecting victim is about to be strangled to death or knifed in the shower.

Leigh grabbed my arm and escorted me into the dining area on the opposite side of the lobby. Seated at a table were four legislators. On my immediate right was Rep. Ralph Wright, a Bennington

[56]

Democrat. On my left was Rep. Alexander "Bud" Keefe, whom I had met the night before at the poker game. He gave me a big smile. Across the table was Rep. Tom Candon wearing his trademark, camel-hair blazer. I don't remember who the fourth person was.

Ralph Wright had a wry grin on his face, which at the time I didn't understand, but later figured out. He was grinning with amusement that Tofferi had hooked up with this young Republican and managed to get him hammered on the second day of the session. I shook hands with Ralph and the other man. I smiled and shook hands with "Keefer," as he was also known. Keefer had a firm handshake and always a big, warm smile on his face. I reached across the table to shake hands with Mr. Candon.

It was here things got a little dicey. I reached across the table (it was a freakin' miracle that I didn't keep going and fall right onto the table), hand extended. Mr. Candon was sawing away at his steak. He looked up at me, slightly nodded his head, and kept sawing, thus leaving my hand hanging out there like a piece of laundry on a clothesline.

Whatever it is that swims around in this twisted brain of mine chose this moment to surface. "What's up with that?" I thought to myself. "That guy just snubbed me. He's no better than me. We're both elected. This guy just snubbed me? What the hell?" The smart play was to retract the hand as though nothing happened and leave. I've oftentimes wondered how things would have turned out if just once I opted for the smart play.

What's the protocol? Do I slap this guy? Shout at him? Nope. Best to maintain composure. I looked at the small vase of daisies and baby's breath flowers in the center of the table and then at Mr. Wright.

"Are you using these?" I asked as I pointed to the flowers. A look of bewilderment came over Ralph's face, "Uh, no, I don't think so," he said in his thick Boston accent.

I reached over and yanked the flowers out of the vase and began eating them. Chomping and chewing away, stems and all. At one point there was a real risk I might choke to death on the stems, which would have most certainly embellished the point I was trying to make. With my voice cracking a bit due to the stems lodged in my windpipe, I pointed to the little piece of steak that remained on Ralph's plate. "You gonna eat that?" I asked.

His smile widening a bit, and cautiously backing away from the table slightly, he said, "No."

I grabbed the piece of steak with my right hand and took a bite out of it. There was a little gristle left, which I dropped back on the plate. I grabbed the corner of the tablecloth and wiped my hands. The expression on their faces looked like something out of a Norman Rockwell painting. Wide eyes. Mouths gaping frozen in time.

Leigh had me by my left arm saying something like, "Uh, we gotta go now." I wasn't done. I reached across the table for a second time with my now greasy right hand lunging into Mr. Candon's face.

"The name's STANNARD. BOB STANNARD. Pleased to meet you."

The silverware that was clenched between thumbs and fingers dropped with a clang on the plate. A shaky right hand extended in my direction. "Ccccandon. Tom Candon. Pleased to meet you."

Leigh was successful in dragging me away from the table. Once outside he said, "What the hell was that about? Do you know who those men are? They are some of the most powerful people in Montpelier. You are done here. You are toast," he said.

For a calm guy, Leigh could sometimes overreact. What the hell? I was mowing lawns for a living a few short months ago. Now I'm a Republican legislator, for heaven's sake. Geez, cut a guy a little slack.

"Well, Leigh," I said, "no I don't know those guys, but I can assure you that old guy with the white hair and camel-hair jacket won't forget me for a while, ya think?" Throughout dinner that evening all Leigh could say was that I was done for. My career was over. I suggested he cheer up a little, because he was bumming me out. I have never been in search of a career, say anything of a career in politics.

Oddly enough, we did have another cocktail and I, for one, did NOT feel better. As a matter of fact, when I woke up the next morning, I felt like a pack of rabid dogs had tromped through my mouth on their way to chewing on my brain while I slept. I got up, showered, and went to work. I couldn't take off my sunglasses for fear of at least one of the eyeballs cracking, falling out, and shattering into little pieces on that nice black and white marble floor laden with fossils in the lobby of the State House.

I opened the door to the side entrance, where most people enter the building, and looked down the massive corridor. The black and white marble floor is covered with a wide, red indoor-outdoor carpet. Light pours in from floor to ceiling windows in the lobby. I squinted (because I had no choice in the matter) and lo and behold, who do I see? There stood two men speaking to each other. The man on the left is wearing glasses and was pretty thin. The man on the right with a bit of a round tummy and wearing a camel-hair sports coat was none other than the snubber I had met the night before. Can you guess where this is going?

"Hey, it's a small building. You're going to see this guy at some point. Suck it up and go say hello," said the voice in my head that has been known to get me into more trouble than it has served to avoid pitfalls such as the one I was about to encounter.

I approached the two men. Mr. Candon looked my way. I gulped.

"Hey, Peter. Here's a guy you gotta meet," he said to Peter Guilianni, a Montpelier Republican and Chair of the powerful Ways and Means Committee. (Later I discovered that Candon was Vice Chair of this committee). "Come here, tiger. I want you to meet Peter Guilianni. Peter, this guy is BOB STANNARD. It's best that you remember that name. He's a live wire this one."

Somewhat sheepishly I shook the hand of Peter Guilianni for the first time. Over the next two years we would become good friends. He sat across the aisle from me in the House. Turned out that Leigh's fear of my career going in the toilet was unfounded. I was making friends left and right. This "Politicking" business was really something. Like Dad always said, "You never get a second chance to make a first impression."

Chapter 8

Still More Politics

You know how some folks say, "That guy is 'Old School.' " They don't necessarily mean it in a derogatory sort of way. It's more like he is of the old ways. If you're a Vermonter, you most likely are "Old School."

There was a man in the legislature who was old school. He dressed impeccably. He was cordial and a real gentleman's gentleman. He would never intentionally offend or harm anyone.

I had invested a fair amount of time either in the overstuffed, red leather chairs at the Tavern or the three barstools on the end of the bar where you could sit with your back to the red chairs. This evening in question I was at my favorite seat at the bar.

It was early in the first session of my first year in the legislature, 1983. I considered myself a seasoned pro. I knew where the downstairs, private, all marble, men's bathroom was. I was friends with some pretty influential folks. Well, OK, maybe in some cases they were just afraid of me, but they acted in a friendly way toward me.

The Speaker of the House was Stephen Morse from Newfane; an intense man with piercing eyes. Lee Marvin eyes. A cold stare from the Speaker would cause weaker members to crap in their pants right on the spot. At times I considered wearing a diaper just for insurance.

The Speaker's mother had been quite ill and early into the session succumbed to the horrible disease of cancer. Nearly the entire General Assembly attended the funeral. I don't much like funerals and I couldn't see any reason to go to a funeral for someone I did not know for any other reason than to suck up to the Speaker. The funeral was on a Friday. I didn't go.

The following Tuesday I was sitting at the bar with my friend and roommate, Leigh Tofferi, and our old school friend. I don't recall if Leigh went to the funeral, but I do know that our friend went.

He's Irish. It provided him with an opportunity to cry and sing and the Irish love to cry and sing. As a Blues singer I get this.

We're sitting at the bar when in walks Speaker Morse and his entourage. When you are the Speaker or an otherwise prominent politician you acquire an entourage. Your entourage generally is comprised of suck ups that will buy you drinks and make sure you get a good seat at the tavern. The Speaker and company took over the red chairs.

Here I am, a Republican, sitting at the bar between two Democrats. We're sipping away when our "Old School" friend looks at both of us and declares, "Boys, please excuse me. I must have a word with the Speaker."

Whoa. No kidding? There was no good reason for him to have a word with the Speaker. It wasn't like the Speaker disliked him. No one did, but no Speaker ever wants to talk with anyone, really. Unfortunately for Speaker Morse, the option of not speaking with him was, well, not an option.

Elegantly, yet cautiously he turned to his right on the bar stool. He was facing me. His eyes were probably as glassy as my own, but I couldn't see my eyes. He turned another ninety degrees and is now on his feet. Leigh and I are simultaneously proud of his display of dexterity and anxious that he's on his feet.

Ramrod straight. Pocket silk hanging out of his suit coat pocket just exactly the right amount. His hair looked like a silver flag unfurling in the wind. His shoes glistened. He was a sight to behold. As he approached the Speaker the entourage was appropriately nervous. "What's he doing over here" is written on each of their faces. None of the entourage or the Speaker had yet removed their sleek, black, woolen overcoats. The Speaker had a signature cigarette dangling precariously in the right corner of his mouth. Yes, there was a time that smoke-filled barrooms not only existed, but were the norm. This was that time.

[63]

He stood before the Speaker who remained seated. He then bent down on one knee, much like he would when genuflecting prior to taking his seat in the pew at his hometown church. The Speaker's stare was enough to boil my bourbon and water. I placed my hand over the drink, just in case. Our friend was not fazed in the least by the powerful stare, presumably because his own eyes were protected by a glassy film. His rye and sodas might be saving him here. Unfortunately this was not to be the case. Instead, he thought it best to speak. Bad idea.

"Mr. Speaker. How is your mom?" he asked the Speaker.

"She's dead," the Speaker replied with stony disbelief. A Tsunami wave of recall washed over our friend. If one looked carefully, and oh by the Jeezus, we were all looking carefully, you might have noticed the slightest twinge rifle up and down his body. Without saying a word, he arose from bended knee. His back perfectly straight, eyes looking straight ahead. He turned 180 degrees and began walking toward us at the bar. He approached his vacated seat, turned around, placed his butt on the stool, and slowly pivoted around and faced the bar.

You could have heard a fly fart out on State Street. Those who witnessed this marvel were as dumbstruck as if the Virgin Mary had come in and ordered free dinner and drinks for everyone at the bar.

"I think another rye and soda is in order here when you get a chance" were the next words he spoke. It might not have been his best line, but it broke the ice.

Even if we are in the best of times (a rarity in Vermont), it's generally not a good idea to do too much of a good thing.

Chapter 9

Typical Vermont Family Values

To successfully steer clear of the negative impacts of a recession it's essential to have strong family values. Occasionally friends of mine will say to me, "You know, Bob, you are one crazy son-of-a-bitch." Naturally, I assume that they mean this in the most affectionate of terms. People older than I am will say, "Well, you're crazy, but you're not nearly as crazy as your father." Hearing this generally causes my body temperature to drop a few degrees, because A, they probably knew him, and B, they have a story about him.

My Dad was an interesting character. He was a plumber. He worked for his dad, who started a plumbing company after deciding that farming, as a way to make a living, sucked. Farmers today have come to the same conclusion. Our family was always grateful that my grandfather figured it out early on.

My dad graduated from the same high school as I did, Burr and Burton Seminary, which is now known as Burr and Burton Academy. It is no longer a school for those hoping to go into the ministry. I believe my dad may have been responsible for that. High school was as far as he got in formal education. However, he had his doctorate in life education. He was Magna Cum Freakin' Laude in living life.

As long as I can remember he read a book a day. Every day. Every week. Every month. All year. Trashy novels for the most part, but not always. When I was growing up he read more books than anyone I ever knew. He was gregarious and to quote my old friend, Charlie Buchmayr, "You're pretty funny, Bob, but you're not nearly as funny as your father." Never one to get too carried away on a compliment, that Charlie.

"What was it that made my dad such fun to be around," you ask? Well, before I continue, let's take a moment to remember what this book is about. It's about a Vermont perspective on how to make it through a recession, right? This is important, because the things that go on in Vermont are not like the things that go on in, say, Las Vegas. OK, so maybe card playing IS involved, but we don't do

[66]

the flashy lights, bells and whistles here. NO FLASHY LIGHTS. Well, OK, maybe some flashy lights. Not lights like Vegas, but more like the flash of fire from the business end of a rifle.

Life's different here than where you live. This book is important, because it will help you to better understand things, like how Vermont can have a Republican majority in the House of Representatives yet elect a Democrat as Speaker (that's what happened to that Ralph Wright guy I spoke about earlier).

We can elect a huge Democratic majority in both the House AND the Senate yet elect a Republican Governor. We're the first state to have its legislature adopt gay marriage. We're the "whitest" state in the nation, yet the first state in the country to vote for a black President. We're different. We also have a thing about money. We tend not to spend it if we don't have it. An ancient rule handed down by elders.

Much like Vermont, my dad was a little different. In a good way. He was slightly, let me see, how do I say this—WILD. There are many stories still floating around southern Vermont today about my dad. I work hard to squelch them whenever I can, but it's a lot like trying to kill ants.

To stress the importance of family values and how they can positively impact your chances of surviving the recession I will share this event with you. The year was 1965. My parents had recently purchased their first new car, a 1965 Ford LTD. My Mom loved this car. It was medium blue and longer than many houses in my neighborhood. We were not rich, but somehow they had been able to scrape up enough money to purchase this car. Let it suffice to say that it was a big deal in our household as well as the neighborhood.

The car was still new that winter when the Vermont Legislature was debating a doe season bill. Now, for those of you who are not from Vermont, it's doe season; not dough season. We've never had the latter here in Vermont.

In any case, doe season is when you get to shoot female deer right along with the males during the sacred two weeks of deer season, beginning the second Saturday of November. "What's the big deal?" you ask. You would only say that because you don't know much about Vermont and/or Vermonters when it comes to deer season.

Number one – Vermonters do not, let me repeat, DO NOT believe in shooting does. Alright, let me rephrase that. They DO NOT believe in shooting does during the regular season in November. They would prefer to jack them in July. My friends from Manhattan have no idea what the term "jacking" means so let me help you out here. You "shoot" a deer during the regular season. You "jack" a deer any other time of the year. Yes, "jacking" a deer is highly illegal and no one I know, have ever known, or will ever know in the future has ever jacked a deer or even thought about jacking a deer. It's never happened. We've only heard about it through talk at the diner.

Nothing arouses anger in the Vermont male more than the prospect of a doe season. "It just ain't right" you will hear them say. They will get pretty animated about the idea, too. If you don't think so, go to a Fish and Wildlife public hearing on the issue. Some advice: sit in the back of the room, keep your hands down, don't speak, don't make eye contact.

OK, back to the story. My dad was driving the new Ford LTD. In the car was his brother, Johnny, and Johnny's son, Jack. One of my dad's best friends when he was growing up was Terry Tyler (another well-known local author and former constable). Dad, Terry, and Johnny were in the front seat. Jack, my brother, Jimmy, and I were in the back seat.

We pulled into the State House and drove right through it. There was a time up until a few years ago that you could drive right through this above ground tunnel that took you right through the State House. It has since been blocked off. Terrorists, ya know.

[68]

Fear has screwed up just about everything, including being able to drive through the State House.

Anyway, we parked in this small parking area and went into the Vermont House of Representatives. It was my first time in the Montpelier State House. Growing up in South Dorset in the 1950s and '60s pretty much meant that you didn't do much and you didn't ever go anywhere. Going to Rutland was a real big deal. We did that about every other month, presumably to keep from losing our minds. Montpelier? Well, you'd only go there for a Fish and Wildlife public hearing.

For about four hours we listened to every sportsman from every corner of the state talk about the ills of killing doe during the regular season. Astonishingly, not one person testified that this legislation pass. Most feared the unintended consequences could be a heavy, negative impact on jacking deer in July. Vermonters, oftentimes, like to keep some of their thoughts and opinions on jacking to themselves. This was one of those times.

To quote a man with whom I would later serve in the legislature, Rep. Cola Hudson, "Everything's been said, but not everyone has said it."

Four hours is about all any stalwart human being can take hearing about the pros and cons of killing anything, so we decided it was about time to depart this historic structure where two decades later I would serve as a State Representative.

We're in the new, 1965 Ford LTD ready to head back down south. My dad starts to pull out of the parking area and go back the way we came only to see a sign that read "ONE WAY." He turned the car around, which consisted of approximately a 32-point turn taking roughly half an hour, only see that the other apparent exit also had a sign that read "ONE WAY."

[69]

Man, what are the odds. Only two ways out and both are one way the wrong way. Now my dad was never one for breaking the law (OK, those of you who are reading this and knew my father, just be quiet now), at least when he was out of town and didn't know the local cops.

He was penned in and I bet feeling somewhat claustrophobic. Maybe he had a flashback from World War II, but who knows. All I know is that what happened next was something we'd never forget.

Somewhat under his breath he mumbled, "By God, I can get out of here," and turned the car downhill toward the steps of the State House. If you are standing on State Street looking up at the beautiful building with the golden dome you would look to your left. Had you been standing there on this particular night in 1965 you would have seen a medium blue Ford LTD with a dark blue top, with six passengers fly across the grass towards the front of the building and then turn right and head toward State Street; right down the dozens of granite steps that lead to State Street. You would have been amused or, depending on where you were standing…frightened.

We, on the other hand, were not amused. We were all bouncing around inside the car like kids in one of those blow-up rooms that look like a giraffe at the county fair. Stuff was flying everywhere. We were banging around, crashing into each other. Somewhere along the line we left the exhaust system behind us and the car took on a very onerous tone. Amazingly we made it to State Street.

The two-hour drive home was interesting. No one spoke, because you couldn't hear yourself speak, because the new Ford LTD sounded slightly louder than a stock car at Devil's Bowl Speedway in Fair Haven on a hot summer night. We made it back to Dorset. We dropped off my uncle and cousin. We dropped off Terry Tyler. We got about two hundred yards from our house when our

[70]

father turned off the ignition key. The deafening roar of the car went stone cold silent.

Although not an engineer, Dad was one crafty son-of-a-gun. He had timed it perfectly so that we coasted right into the driveway and right into the garage. He put the shifter lever into park and on came the dome light, but no doors opened. My father's right arm gently lay on the top of the *ginormous* (a word I have picked up from my daughter, Meredith, meaning really big) front seat and he turned around to face his two sons.

Dad looked us both in the eyes for an exceedingly long period of time before saying, "Now boys, I don't see any merit in sharing the events of this evening with your mother, do you?"

Had we been able to speak I have no doubt that we both would have said, "Why no, Dad. Of course not." Instead, we responded with a nervous twitch that he interpreted as "NO. No need to say anything about anything."

Now, this sordid little tale should be about over, but you should know by now that you're not that lucky. The next morning, after my dad had left for work (his office was diagonally across the street from our house), my mom went out to take the car into town to do some shopping. I did not have the benefit of seeing her face when she started the car.

Mom was part German and part Swedish. She had the reddest hair of any human that ever lived. It was perfect. In times such as the one I am describing her hair color uncannily matched her temper. You knew that she had started her new car if you had been in the next county over. She went ballistic. She ran inside and called my dad who was presumably awaiting the call. Before she could begin screaming at him, which he had anticipated, he immediately cut her off. "Take the car down to Power's Auto Body Shop, Thyra. They're waitin' for you."

[71]

That was Dad. Always thinkin' ahead. I learned a lot about marital bliss watching those two in action. Fortunately, I have never opted to implement any of the knowledge I garnered from Dad. That explains why I'm still here and able to write this book. I still have my fingers. That's a good thing.

Jim Stannard was a pretty open-minded guy. It just took a while for this to become clear to me, that's all.

One at a Time

When I was about 9 or 10 years old I was grocery shopping with my mom at the IGA in Manchester. You know the former store's location as that of Rt. 11/30; approximately where Polo resides today.

We had made our rounds in the small, quaint "supermarket" and were headed to the checkout counter where Anna Giddings would ring up our items. Bearing down hard on our left was a lady from "down country" who roughly cut right in front of my mom.

Although Mom had quite a temper when it came to me and my brother, she seemed remarkably reserved as the lady in the expensive coat and makeup barged in front of us. Mom never said a word.

Later that evening we were sitting around our dinner table when my dad asked how our day went. Again, Mom was silent about the experience at the IGA. Her silence caused me to speak up at the dinner table saying, "There was a real asshole from New Jersey who cut in front of us at the grocery store today." Mom almost dropped her silverware, shocked at hearing the account of the incident and doubly shocked, I think, that I would dare swear at the dinner table. I could feel her [something missed here? "glaring"?] across the table from me.

My dad never flinched at my inflammatory adjective. Instead, he calmly placed his silverware down on his plate and gave me a very

[72]

contemplative look. "You say this lady was from New Jersey?" he asked.

"Yes, she had to be. She wasn't from around here," I replied.

"And you say she was an asshole?" he inquired. I was somewhat confused at how he could not have readily comprehended that of course she was an asshole. I nodded my head in reply.

"So, we can conclude that all people from New Jersey are, therefore, assholes," he stated. I could now see what a brilliant man he was as he was honing in on my astute conclusions perfectly.

"Yes," I replied.

He picked up his knife and fork, carved off a little piece of steak, and chewed it carefully, almost with complete conviction as he stared at me. It was not an intimidating and/or scolding stare, but one that seemed to be more of an awakening, like he was seeing the answers to the universe. He was getting it. All people from New Jersey are assholes. We were in perfect sync.

"Well," he said, "I guess you could see it that way, but I don't think I would." Say what? He appeared to be going astray. How could he not see it that way? This was the ONLY way to see it. I was positive of my position and couldn't believe that he could now be abandoning me at this time. "I prefer to let people demonstrate to me, one at a time, that they're assholes instead of letting the actions of one define an entire state."

Oh man, I had been tossed overboard. I couldn't believe it. How could he be so dumb? The lady was rude, obnoxious and aggressive. She had to be from New Jersey. People from other places don't act like this. I had heard from my other 10-year-old friends that people from New Jersey were jerks. She fit the profile. What was Dad not getting? How could he possibly turn on me like this?

[73]

As time went on, I frequently thought about that moment. The image of this man, who was a plumber, a blue-collar kind of guy, a beer-and-steak guy, is always with me. I have asked myself how and why this man ended up being such a visionary; a man of great tolerance. Perhaps it was handed down from generations or maybe it was where and how he was raised. Whatever it was, I have come to appreciate how lucky I was to have been handed this lesson at such an early age.

I shared this story with my own children when they were around 10 years old. I don't know if it had the same impact; I doubt it did, but it was important to share it.

I should also mention that I was eternally grateful that my mom showed great restraint and opted not to wash my mouth out with soap!

April 15, 2007

Here is how those words affected me in later life. You may recall that Don Imus got pitched off the air for what some thought to be a racial slur. The following is a column I wrote on his departure.

IMUS

"Nappy headed 'ho." Three words that now serve as a bullet to the forehead of a thirty- year radio career.

On Friday the 13th I learned that CBS has followed suit with NBC and cancelled Don Imus's longstanding radio talk show. Many are rejoicing in this decision. Don't count me in with the chorus of voices that were calling for his head.

No, I do not condone what he said. He admittedly went over the top, but to his credit he immediately recognized his lame mistake, apologized and accepted responsibility. There is no question that a penalty deserved to be invoked and tossing him off the airwaves might have been justified if all were held accountable to the same standard.

It was Easter weekend when we learned of the furor caused by the utterance of these three words. I was sitting in my living room with my future son-in-law, who is an African American, and I asked him for his thoughts. He said, "Until the blacks of this nation stop using derogatory words toward themselves, it's unfair for them to get up in arms if others do the same." You can see why I am honored to have this young man in my family.

We talked about how the black leaders of this country don't appear to mind if Chris Rock uses the "N-word" in his HBO specials, or if Dave Chappell refers to black women as "bitches and 'ho's." No one seems to mind that Carlos Mencia trashes Mexican rights along with everyone else. These guys are comedians trying to be funny. The only apparent difference is that these guys are black and Mexican.

The world got angry at Michael Richards, formerly of "Seinfeld," for screaming at a heckler and calling him by the "N-word." Richards wasn't trying to be funny and paid a price. Ann Coulter, last year in a speech before the Conservative Political Action Conference, referred to Muslims as "ragheads." And what was this nationally syndicated columnist's reprimand for this venomous racial attack? She was invited back before the same group this year in which she referred to gay people as "faggots." Coulter was not trying to be funny. Her columns still run nationwide.

The infamous "Denmark cartoons" disparaged the Muslim prophet, Mohammed. The Islamic radical Muslim community publishes cartoons lampooning Christians and Jews, but when the situation was reversed, they rioted, went on a rampage, threatened, burned things, screamed and shouted. Americans watched as we would watch a two-year-old freak out in the grocery store and thought their reaction was way over the top.

[75]

Don Imus has been doing a mix of comedy and serious interviews four hours a day, five days a week for over thirty years, during which times he lays claim to receiving a record five Marconi Awards. His show is by design, edgy, which explains his large following. Peter Crabtree, a fine reporter and photographer for this paper, convinced me to tune into Imus a decade ago. I'm glad he did.

There have been times when Imus's biting comments have made me wince, but I don't believe Don Imus is a bigot. He has done a lot of good raising millions for charities, including his own working ranch for kids with cancer. I realize that just because he raises money doesn't mean he couldn't be a bigot. I've concluded he is not a bigot by listening to his show.

A man who has raised millions for the "Fallen Heroes Fund" and the "Sudden Infant Death Syndrome" foundation can now no longer do so, but you can feel free to tune into HBO or Comedy Central and watch a black man or a Mexican, in good fun, denigrate their respective races. I think I would feel better about all of this if the Chris Rocks of the world would stand up for Don Imus, but as a line in one of the songs I sing goes, "When a man has his troubles, everybody throws him down." Leaving him on the air, after a hiatus, to carry on a national dialog about words and race would have served a purpose. Instead, we have now swept that debate right under the rug along with Imus.

I guess if we're willing to accept double standards, then we should be OK with the firing of Don Imus. But I'm not "OK" with it. If he has to go, so should many others on the air and in the print media. The firing of Don Imus is as over-the-top a reaction as that of the Muslims to a cartoon, and conversely, as the deafening silence of the black community toward its own.

April 14, 2007

Chapter 10

Lessons Learned the Hard Way

In times of a recession it's always wise to play your cards close to your vest. If you find a way to make a buck or two, it's a good idea to keep it to yourself. The key to surviving a recession is very similar to playing a good hand in a card game—cautiously.

My father was a tolerant man, with one exception—fooling around while playing cards. Along with reading a book a day, he played cards nearly every day. Any card game would do. Poker, cribbage (that was a big one), Pitch. He knew them all and he was a pretty darn good player at all of them.

His friends never did know if he was clairvoyant or had an ability to count cards. Inevitably, at some point in a card game with Jim Stannard one would witness a little stunt that he liked to pull. You would put your fingers on the next card you were about to lay down on the table but before you could draw it out, he would say, "You're not really thinking of playing the queen of spades are you?" That would be the card between your thumb and index finger. It was unnerving.

He didn't do this often, but he never had to. It was spooky for anyone playing against him. That's not to say he won all the time. He just drove his opponents crazy. I credit him for my ability to do likewise.

I was 17, which means it would have been 1968. Now, in the likely event that you have already forgotten why this book is being written—to help all of you folks from down country to better understand the workings of the small, yet great State of Vermont, as well as how to survive a recession—I will remind you to pay close attention.

It was a hot summer night and my father, Jim, my older brother, Jimmy, and I all attended the local Dorset Sportsman's Club monthly meeting. The meetings typically lasted until about 9:00 p.m. at which time most of the club members, those with an acute sense of marital survival, scurried home. Then there were the others. The Card Players.

[78]

There were eight of us playing Pitch that night. For you poor souls not familiar with this odd little card game, it's one in which you play a suit. Points are scored by acquiring the highest card in the suit as declared by the player who wins the bid. Six cards are dealt. Each player has the option of discarding up to three cards. Once this has been completed the bidding begins with the player on the dealer's right. We would leave both jokers in the deck. Each joker counted as one point. Points went as follows: Highest card of the suit. Lowest card of the suit. The jack of the suit and then all of the other cards from 10 on up would be counted for what was called "the game." Add in two jokers and the maximum one could bid would be six. You better have a darned good hand to bid six.

The bid can be increased to any level by any player in the rotation. The dealer does not have to raise the bid but can take it for the last bid made. Here's where things got sticky on this hot July evening.

My father was a master card player, but didn't need to be for this particular round. The cards had been dealt and players issued new cards after discarding those they didn't want. Dad did not discard a single card in this round. That made everyone very nervous. Next, he did the unconscionable. He leaned forward as I leaned backward, allowing me the opportunity to peak at his hand.

I should mention here that every other player at the table is on a team. There are two teams with four players to a team. I was not on my Dad's team. Unfortunately for both men, my dad's best friend, Ed Tarbell, was on his team and just so happened to be the dealer.

I sneaked a quick peak at my father's hand. He had played cards almost every day of his life and yet had never been dealt a Royal Straight Flush...until that moment. There they were in all their glory: the ace, king, queen, jack, and 10 of hearts, joined by a trash card, the 4 of spades.

Now dad could have bid six; no, make that SHOULD have bid six on this once-in-a-lifetime hand, but he had experienced some hard living early in life. He was pretty conservative. There was one other player between him and his best friend Ed, who was also the dealer, and that was his brother, Johnny. If there was ever anyone more conservative than Jim, it was Johnny. Jim just knew his brother would not bid six and he also knew that there would never be a scenario on earth where his own partner, his best friend, his dealer, would ever take away a 5-bid from him.

There have been only a few times when my dad did not fully anticipate the situation in which he found himself. Leaving the Vermont State House was one. Bidding 5 on what was legitimately a 6-bid hand was another. After announcing he would bid 5, he turned to look at his brother, who, predictably, had no desire to bid six. All eyes were now on Ed Tarbell.

Before I continue I should mention that it was now almost midnight. We had been playing cards for about three hours. Earlier in the evening as we began playing cards, we had a pot of exquisite venison stew my dad made. I'm sure that the venison was frozen and left over from last November, instead of being more recently obtained. We also consumed a fair amount of beer. My brother and I were never allowed to drink, unless we were with our father. We always liked hanging out with Dad.

All eyes are on Ed. "Well, let's see here, Jim. You bid 5. That must mean you have a pretty good hand there, 'cause you don't bid 5 unless you got a pretty good hand," Tarbell declared. Everyone could feel my father's eyes on Ed. "It's not like me to take away a hand from my partner." At this point I couldn't help noticing my father's head moving ever so slightly left and right, clearly signaling to Ed that he was not pleased with what he was hearing.

"I'm real tempted to take it for 5, Jim," and at that point I swear Dad kicked Ed in the shins under the table, because Ed flinched from an unforeseen force. "On the other hand, Jim, I've known you to bluff every now and again." Veins were beginning to show in my father's forehead. His cheeks flushed. "I think I'm gonna take it for 5," and then Ed Tarbell laid out the deuce of clubs, the lowest card of the suit. I had the king and another club and knew that I was in position to set him. To "set" means that if you don't attain the bid, you lose a like amount. Since the game goes only to 21, losing 5 points is not good. Stealing them from Jim Stannard is really, really not good.

The cards were laid out one by one as each player took a turn. The laying of cards progressed until it finally came around to me. I played the low club and saved the King for the next round. The ol' "nail in the coffin" deal. My dad was next. He played his 4 of spades. Sure enough, another one of my teammates had the Ace. Tarbell was sunk on the first go-round.

The next round rolled around to Dad who played the 10 of hearts. Next round, the jack. Next round, the queen. The room was very silent and feeling a little tense. That tension could have been because my dad had not taken his eyes off Ed Tarbell since they began laying down their cards. He knew where each card was in his hand. After all, it was the first and only time in his life he had ever been dealt a Royal Straight Flush and he had to sit there with people he'd known his whole life and watch it slide right away.

Next round, he gently laid the king of hearts down on the table. "Boy, you got yourself a pretty darn good hand there, Jim. Ya know, if you got the ace, boy, I bet you'll be pissed," Ed said. Breaking all the rules of science, my father had not blinked for about 5 minutes. I wondered if perhaps he might be a vampire.

Ed laid down his sixth and final card. Round the table we went and when it stopped at Jim, he placed down the ace of hearts. You'll hear more noise at a hearing impaired convention held at a funeral parlor than there was in that room at that one moment in time.

I will pause right here, because I think it might be helpful to discuss the building in which this event took place. It was known as "The Legion Rooms." This building used to be the Dorset Elementary School. It was the quintessential one-room schoolhouse. It was heated by a giant parlor stove that burned wood. It was always cold unless you sat in the front row, which was reserved for the kids that needed watchin'. I was always pretty warm.

A rope hung from the ceiling. It was used to ring the bell on the roof outside. I'm not making this up. The rope would settle down a few minutes after Miss Jones rang the bell. The same could be said for the kids. For about the next hour of so we would stare at the motionless rope knowing that one false move and it could be quickly tied around one's young, skinny neck. It was a handy tool to advance our education. Miss Jones was pretty handy with another tool—the ruler—and not for measuring.

It was unfair to call this a one-room schoolhouse, as it had a kitchen, of sorts, in the back, left corner. The right corner is where we hung our coats and stored our coats and lunch pails with Roy Rogers and Dale Evans enameled into the finish. It was also where the two-holer-inhouse was located. For those of you who may not be familiar with an "in-house," it's very similar to an outhouse, except that it's inside.

The answer is NO to both questions you're about to ask. NO, we didn't have indoor plumbing that worked in the winter, and thus had to sit on a wooden bench with a circle cut in it where the brave would park their little butts and do their business. And NO, I never sat on the circle, because there was never any doubt in my mind that I would fall into that world's stinkiest pit and never come out alive, and if I did come out alive would most assuredly kill myself (it was hard enough for me to get a date in the later years. The last thing I needed circulating around a small Vermont town is a story that for all eternity would remember me as the kid who fell into the inhouse at Dorset School/Legion Rooms). Suffice it to say that I was always excited to get home from school and use our real indoor plumbing. The year after I left first grade they condemned the building for use as a school. Apparently that

[82]

qualified it to become the American Legion Rooms, though. There's a joke there somewhere.

Interestingly enough, every school I attended for the first three years of my public education experience was condemned immediately upon my departure. When you're skinny (something I was able to overcome as the years went by), towheaded, have freckles, sticky-out ears, goofy teeth, and big feet, it's not impossible to feel somewhat self-conscious when you hear that they've closed another school right behind you on your way out. We learned a lot in those ratty-ass, decrepit, lead-painted, soon-to-be-condemned buildings. Got a fine education, we did. I have no way of knowing but I doubt it cost all that much to educate us. We consider thriftiness a virtue up here in Vermont. Being thrifty prepares you for a recession. As stated in the opening comments of this book, we just assumed we were in one from the get-go. Never really thought much about it. Notwithstanding the possibility of falling into a pretty well-seasoned inhouse pit, I don't think we paid much mind to being in a depressed economy. Of course, we were only six years old. You don't worry about much at six, except for maybe having someone hide your Roy Rogers lunch pail.

Dad never took his eyes off Ed. He slowly rose out of his chair and took three steps to his right where there was a wall about eight feet away. Hanging in a gun rack on the wall was a half-dozen World War I issue 30.06 rifles. They were old school. The stock came within six inches of the end of the barrel. They weighed a ton. The old leather straps were in desperate need of some saddle soap and looked like they might snap right in half if you grabbed onto them.

Not one for taking chances at times like these, Dad grabbed the gun by the stock and just as nonchalantly as a maitre d' of a five-star restaurant seating a party of six, glided back over to his seat. His eyes never left Ed Tarbell.

He leaned back in his chair. He stuffed his right hand into the pocket of his blue jeans. I thought I saw a glint of brass as he removed his hand from his pocket. He pulled the bolt action of the 30.06 back, exposing the chamber of the high-powered rifle. No mistake this time. He slid a brass jacketed bullet into the chamber of this gun, drew the rifle to his shoulder, checked to make sure the safety was OFF, aimed the gun right at the chest of his best friend, Ed Tarbell, and declared, "Tarbell, you have fucked with me for the last time" – BANG!

My ears were ringing; my eyes were burning from the smoke that instantly filled the room. I felt like I was in a Fellini film. In slow motion I looked through the smoky haze at the faces around the room. There was Ed's father, Cliff, with his mouth wide open. There was Ed's uncle Frank with the same face. Old Claude Dern, the artist, was there. He was from France. He remained calm. Everyone else was in shock. They were stunned. The frozen faces reminded me of a Norman Rockwell painting with a Stephen King twist.

"Oh man, Dad just killed Ed Tarbell" were the words that screamed in my head. They were immediately followed by "Well, that dumbass should've known better than to take a 5-bid away from my father. Jeez, Ed's played cards with him longer'n I'd been alive. What the hell was he thinking?"

Thinking it through, the fool had it coming. Dad was completely justified in blowing him away. Perhaps a LITTLE extreme but most certainly justifiable."

Vermonters can rationalize just about anything if it's logical and fair. Ed knew perfectly well that his lifelong friend had a great hand. He also knew that his best friend was going to be pissed. Ed had seen the pissed side of Jim before and thus had some idea that there were consequences to his actions. That said, he probably didn't think he was going to die over it. Well, he should've just thought it through a little more carefully.

A few thousand eternities passed as we all sat there, jaws dropped, mouths gaped open wide enough to park a truck inside. The smoke from the barrel was moving in the air but in slow motion. It appeared to have frozen in midair. Then it began to clear slightly. Tarbell was nowhere to be seen. Maybe this was one of those Chris Angel deals. You know the magician. Maybe the two of them had cooked up this stunt that afternoon. That sure would be a lot easier to explain to Mom.

From the floor we heard the voice of Ed say, "Am I dead, Jim?" "No" was all Jim said. Thankfully that old schoolhouse was so drafty and leaky that it did not explode from the collective exhaling of the six of us who had held our breath for what seemed like a geological time period.

"Jesus, God Almighty," one man said.

"Son-of-a-bitch," said another.

"Hot damn" a third. "You're not dead unless a blank'd kill you, you asshole" were the words that came out of my Dad's mouth. Life was quickly getting back to normal. Ed was not dead. Dad had not lost his mind (at least no more than he had before). "Whew," I thought to myself; then I started thinking about what just happened.

My dad had been carrying around a blank, 30.06 shell in his pocket for what—a day? A week? A month? He had that blank in his pocket and he'd been waiting for just the right time to use it. My Uncle Johnny said to his brother, "You know, Jim, that wasn't funny." Ed peeled open his shirt and right over his heart was a welt about the size of a Vermont Macintosh apple in the second week of September after a summer of a lot of rain. "He could've had a heart attack and died," Johnny said.

"That would have been fine with me," his brother replied.

"Hey, Jim. I don't blame you. Dang, I had it coming. I should've known better. Boy, you really had me there for a minute. I wouldn't't'a blamed you though," Ed said nervously, yet grateful to

[85]

still be in the game, so to speak. You see, there is a certain degree of understanding that exists between the people of Vermont. We are not above screwing up. We do it all the time. We even know when we do wrong and if and when we're caught at doing wrong and appropriately punished, we're fine with that. While shooting a man over a card game may seem extreme, it had been the way of my father's grandfather, and his grandfather's grandfather. At least over the generations my dad had the good sense to use a blank.

Ed knew he'd done Jim wrong, and having the crap scared right out of him seemed appropriate since it was such a good hand, after all. It's February 2009 as I write this and I can't help thinking that it's too bad my dad's not here to administer some appropriate punishment to Wall Streeters who have done more damage in the past few months than all Vermonters combined for the last eight generations…and that's saying something.

You may recall this is a book about how you, too, can survive a recession by acquiring a better understanding of life in Vermont. They say, "Patience is a virtue." If that's true, then my father had a lot of virtue. Carry a 30.06 bullet in one's pocket for god knows how long, waiting for the right opportunity to come along, takes a lot of patience. Jim Stannard, Sr., had a lot of virtues. He held them closer to his chest than his next hand of cards. He was an alright guy. Just don't screw with him in a card game.

Well, that little piece of excitement served to bring an end to the card game. We all pitched in and cleaned up the place. It was understood without ever mentioning it that Dad would take the rifle home, clean it, and return it to the Legion Rooms later in the week. We got in our respective cars and headed home.

We pulled into the Stannard household's driveway and into the garage. On came the dome light, yet no doors opened. Dad's big right arm was draped over the bench seat that could easily accommodate four people. He turned around about 180 degrees and looked at his two sons, who, although they were slightly older now, still were frozen in fear. "I don't think that there is any merit is sharing the events of this evening with your mother, now do you?"

With cracking vocal chords, my brother and I replied in unison, "Uh, no Dad." All was right with the world. At least the exhaust system was intact on the car. That was a good thing.

Chapter 11

Fitting In

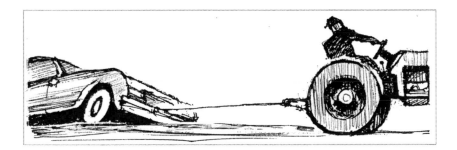

I'm beginning to wonder whether or not you deserve another chapter. Is there any hope that the message of how to survive the recession is sinking in at all? I appreciate how hard this must be for you, not being a Vermonter and all, but think about us for a minute. It's hard enough living here if you are a Vermonter; one who was born here. Someone who has "kin in the ground," as they say. (That would be prior generations who came to grips with the reality that the best way to survive tough times is to reside six feet underground. We're told it's like living on the equator, only cooler.)

We have covered some good ground on how to live in Vermont in these darkest of times. I have heard that the times are dark because Brian Williams of the "Nightly News" has told me so each and every night for the past three months. Thank God for the news guys. Were it not for them Vermonters would have no clue that we are going down the drain. Most Vermonters believe that this state has been in a depression since 1790 (thirty years after the first Stannard arrived in Dorset. There is no connection between the two. It cannot be proven that the Stannards are responsible for the eternal doldrums plaguing the world. Frankly, we believe it was the Bush family that started it all. I just thought it might be helpful for you to know that we were one of the first Official Flatlanders and damn proud of it. I would wager that they shot the guy who called them Flatlanders; probably not with blanks).

Economically speaking, Vermont does not do that great, but it does not do that badly, either. We don't have the peaks and valleys or wild stock swings that other states do (unless you consider a cow that has got into the apples and had them ferment in its stomach, causing it to become intoxicated and stagger off to one side as a stock swing).

You, on the other hand, have probably been raking it in, managing a hedge fund or working a "Bernie Madoff" Ponzi scheme. Those are very complicated jobs and well beyond the mental capacity of any Vermonter's ability to figure out. We're a simple people.

[89]

Screwing an entire city's worth of people out of $50 billion is something that we just can't quite get our heads around.

However, since you are most likely too broke to buy a real book and had to scrape together your last few pennies to buy this book, we can assume that your job at Lehman Bros. is pretty much over. You have probably lost everything. You are going to have to live in a barely adequate home (if you're lucky) or worse. You will be clipping coupons and may be eligible for food stamps.

A Vermonter would assess your new situation and conclude that if you weren't so well off, you could almost be a Vermonter. Rest assured, if you come crawling home to Vermont, after losing everything, expecting a little sympathy, man you're in for a surprise. That you had any money to begin with would be enough to turn off most Vermonters. But we're a forgiving lot. All you need to do is weave yourself into the fabric of our community. Or live in a cave, whatever you find more acceptable.

"How do I work myself into the community?" you ask. First off, not stealing a 5-bid away from a local would be a good place to start, but it'll be a while before you get invited to a card game. Going off the road is always a good place to start. Vermonters thrive on opportunity and opportunity usually runs amuck here in the winter. People come up here in really nice cars with all-season tires. (The all-season tire is good for only one season—summer. In Vermont you should expect to find a $300 car with $800 REAL SNOW TIRES on it.)

At the first dusting of snow, you will most likely go off the road. Now, if you are one of THOSE who don't care to weave your sorry self into the fabric of the community, but instead just take the whole damn cloth and drape it over your head so that no one will see you, that's fine. Life will always be hard for you. Stop reading right now and go do something else. We wish you the best of luck in your other endeavors, but we know deep down to our very core that there is little or no hope for you.

OK, we're going to assume that you want to move here for all the right reasons and hope that by the time your great-great grandchild is born that your family will have been accepted into the community. Now's the time to start paving that road and best way to do that is to drive off it. Try to get yourself stuck just enough so that you can be pulled out with a truck as opposed to having to call the likes of Gen. Petraeus with a division of tanks to yank you out. As my father-in-law likes to remind us of what his father used to say, "There's a difference between scratchin' your ass and tearin' it to pieces." That's a damn good quote considering it's not from a Vermonter.

You see, you need to get stuck just enough on the one hand, and be humble enough to ask for help on the other. Once stuck, stand out on the side of the road and look somewhat forlorn, but don't look like a wimp. That'll cost you a bundle. Look as though this sort of thing happens to you all the time and that you thoroughly expect someone to twitch you out. At some point in time, a Vermonter will drive by in a pickup truck and pull over. You will immediately think that this is a Good Samaritan who has come to help you.

You'd be half right. He'll help you out alright, but there will be a price to pay. Not a lot of cash, mind you. Today you can get twitched out for $30 - $40 bucks (cash, of course). However, you will be paying for many years to come. You'll pay whenever you stop by the local store or gas station and see the guys hanging around snickering at you, because they will know every sordid detail of your misfortune. When this happens it is always best to go on the offensive.

The next time you see the man who pulled you out, you better go say "Hi" and express your extreme gratitude. He will still think you're a moron for going off the road, but those feelings will be washed away by the two six-packs of beer he bought. It will be like a Pavlovian thing. He will see you and think, "That dumbbell went off the road. He wasn't even all that stuck. Probably could'a got out by himself. Didn't put a lick'a strain on my rig and he

[91]

gave me $40 freakin' bucks. That's more than I made all week. He was a pretty good egg."

Only one or two more encounters like this and you'll be asked to go huntin' and snowmobilin' in no time. Here is how not to act once you have arrived.

The View from My Place

I couldn't help but notice some folks in Woodford, Vermont, declaring that they didn't want any more windmills, because they would obstruct the view.

An interesting observation and one I want to understand correctly. We do not want to obstruct or modify the view of our ridgelines with machines that will generate clean, safe electricity from the wind.

However, we will go to war and sacrifice the lives of over 3,000 of our kids so that we can insure that we have enough oil. We will push to re-license an antiquated nuclear power plant that is collapsing before our very eyes and store the most toxic waste known to man in cement caskets that will not last as long as the toxic material it contains.

We will be satisfied with the leveling of mountains; not just a modification of the ridgeline, but a complete removal of a mountain, so that we can get more polluting coal to burn to create electricity.
We don't have any desire to take to the streets in protest over the fact that no president since the last so-called "gas crisis" back in 1973 has done a darn thing about mandating that cars not only get better gas mileage, but get extremely better gas mileage.

We seem to be OK with the idea that a few volunteers should go to Iraq and fight and die so that we can establish an American presence over there to keep track of the oil that we have to have, so we don't impair our view of the mountains.

[92]

We appear willing to accept the fact that California is ablaze with one of the worst fires in history and that New Orleans was destroyed by a hurricane of unprecedented proportions. Has it gone unnoticed that for the first time in Vermont, the tamarack trees are turning at the same time as the hardwood trees? Unbelievable.

The polar ice caps are melting at an alarming rate, much faster than any scientist predicted. In all likelihood the ice caps are melting because of global warming, which is caused by too much carbon in the atmosphere. Carbon comes from burning stuff like fossil fuels. The way to stop creating carbon is to stop burning fossil fuels. The way to stop burning fossil fuels is to immediately, not tomorrow, but TODAY kind of immediately, start investing in sustainable energy sources. Sources that will not result in more problems than they are trying solve.

Nuclear looks good as long as you are willing to discount the fact that the material, uranium, has to be mined, processed and shipped. Then, of course, after it has been burned it is toxic for somewhere between 100,000 and 500,000 years. Do you really want to store this stuff in dry cask storage on the banks of the Connecticut River in Vermont? Maybe. It won't obstruct your view.

I want to be sure that I am hearing these concerns correctly. We don't want our view impacted with wind turbines, because that is not why we moved to Vermont. Will they ruin tourism? Is that it? If so, I would ask how many more calamities at the Entergy Nuclear Plant in Vernon do we need before we discourage tourists from coming here? Will tourists continue to come here if they were to find out that we have a nuclear waste dump on the banks of the Connecticut River?

The simple fact is that we have to get a grip here. We are going to have to come to terms with our lifestyle. We don't want to hear that, but we have no choice. At some point we are going to run out of oil or burn so much of it that the planet will revolt and wipe us

[93]

out. Remember, we are the problem. There is not a problem with the planet. The planet will correct itself over time. Our job is to figure out how to survive.

If we could make a positive contribution to the reduction of global warming and/or the discontinuance of nuclear power and its toxic residue by lining every mountaintop in Vermont with wind turbines, then we should consider doing so. The fact is that we do not have to do this to replace the Entergy plant.

Now I know this is going to make a bunch of you really angry and I'm OK with that. I would rather that you are angry and I still have a planet on which to live, even if that means my view is impaired.

I marvel at the shortsightedness exhibited. It reminds me of someone more concerned with rearranging the deck furniture on the Titanic than changing course. Can you not see what is going on around us? We are sending our kids into battle to secure a resource that, once used, may contribute to our demise. As we push for more nuclear power we learn that the mountain in Nevada (certainly not Vermont) where we were hoping to store the waste recently had an earthquake that rocked their world.
As an eighth-generation Vermonter, I find it difficult to process the logic. We are faced with perhaps the most monumental threats to our survival in history and as we try to fight for the survival of our planet, we hear a handful of folks scream that they don't want their view ruined. For the record, if it will mean that my great, great, great grandchildren might have a planet on which to live, feel free to alter the view from my place.

October 23, 2007

Chapter 12

Flatlander Fits In

Not all folks who move to Vermont have trouble. If you're wicked rich and hire locals to mow your lawn and do your own plumbing, we like you almost immediately. If you don't pay us for our work, then go back and re-read the piece on the card game; then think "live ammo."

There was a lady whose ancestors moved to Manchester. Her family was that of Abraham Lincoln. Go figure. A guy from Illinois finding his way all the way to Vermont. Heard we had a great economy, I bet.

Well, they came here anyway and built a nifty little summer place. They called it Hildene. I would have loved to been around then to hear the locals down at the feed store. I bet they could be overheard saying, "What the hell is a Hildene?" "Dunno, but they're gonna hire me to do the lawn." They immediately liked a Hildene, whatever it was, and hoped more were on the way.

The place was built by railroad baron Robert Todd Lincoln. Close enough to Abraham so it counts. His great (or maybe two greats) granddaughter was a woman named Peggy Beckwith. She was single and rich and on occasion could be fun. Go Google her if you want to hear the public stories about her. The following are somewhat less public stories. Most believe that the Lincoln family was recession proof.

Peggy was a larger-than-life character. In the early 1960s she bought a brand-new pea green, twelve-cylinder German car called a Duesenberg only to trade it in at Leo's Motors for a new Chrysler a short while later. Moving here and doing things like that instantly make you a larger-than-life character. You don't even have to slide off the road and be rescued to be accepted into the community, either. I had two experiences with her that might be worth sharing with you.

I was 16 in the summer of 1967. I was working for my dad during the summer vacation or, as I like to refer to it, as doing penance. My parents gave me a credit card. Doesn't sound like much of a big deal, but it was when credit cards had first come out. Few knew what the heck they were. Seemed like free money to me. The big difference between Vermonters and the rest of the world is that 40 years ago we figured out that credit cards do NOT equal free money. Forty years later many still have not come to grips with the fact that at some point after you make a purchase, you have to pay for it. This is not an easy concept for some to comprehend and I appreciate that. Fortunately, I had a father who was able to explain basic economics to me.

As it turns out, economics is pretty simple. Those of you with a $40,000 balance on your VISA card—you need to really focus here. I ran up a $500 gas bill on this credit card. Remember it was 1967. Minimum wage was about $1.40/hr. I had a big bill to pay. What better way to pay off a bill that you owe your parents than to go to work for your dad? Prison comes to mind. I worked all that summer...free. I no longer use credit cards. Lesson learned.

We arrived at the home of Peggy Beckwith at around 8:10 a.m. It was known as Hildene to some, but most locals knew it as Peggy's place. Upon arrival, before any actual work was performed, the entire crew, which consisted of my dad, his unbelievably loyal friend and coworker, Ken Nichols, and me, all had to trot down to the kitchen and place our order for breakfast with Mrs. Hilliard. I never knew her first name. People I know who knew her said she was very nice. Severe is how I would describe her.

Eating (another) breakfast was NOT an option. You HAD to have breakfast and not just tea and toast. We're talking a hungry chuck kind of breakfast. Two eggs, bacon, sausage, ham, home fries, toast, juice, coffee. If you were asked if you wanted a pancake or two, you damn well better say "Sure."

About 45 minutes later, after your second breakfast, it was now time for work. We were ready for a nap, but off we went in search of a leak. We had been called down to the house because as Peggy had reported to my father, who did all of her plumbing, "There's a leak in the ceiling at the bottom of the stairs in the entryway." Dad told her that there was no plumbing at all over that section of the house. "There's a leak. Get down here."

So, off we went in search of a non-leak. Now, when we walked into the place, you could see plain as day that there was a big stain right there in the ceiling. Obviously there was a leak. But my dad knew every square inch of plumbing in that house and if he said there was no plumbing over that ceiling, then there's no plumbing there.

"Well, maybe it's coming from the attic," she offered, and sent Dad and me up to the attic of Hildene to check the cistern that served as the original water supply for the house. It was still full of rainwater on the day that I saw it and ready to operate. I had never seen anything like it. It was large and all copper. It was beautiful; well, except for the dead chipmunk that was floating on the surface. That would sour it for drinking water as far as I was concerned.

Looking around the attic, I could see at least one bust of Abraham. On his white marble head rested his beaver stovepipe hat. It looked a little worn, but there it was; the hat that Abraham Lincoln wore. Or maybe it was Robert's, but either way it was pretty exciting. There were papers strewn around. The place was a bit of a mess. I looked on the floor and saw a check lying there. I bent over to pick it up. It was a check signed by Abraham Lincoln. "This would go nicely into my wallet," I thought to myself, but before doing so I thought I should show it to my father. "Hey, Dad, check this out," and I showed him this little piece of history. We never even thought about it then but that check was probably worth a lot of money.

He looked it over, unimpressed. He'd seen all this stuff before. "Put that right back where you found it. Make sure it is in exactly the same place." (The dust outline made that easy.) What a stick-in-the-mud the old man was. We left the attic without one piece of memorabilia, or having found the leak.

We descended the stairs to the second floor. "Come with me," Dad said. I followed him down a corridor. When he thought he was about over the ceiling in question, he stopped. The door on our right led to one of the historic bedrooms. The door had been cut in half so it was now a Dutch door. The top half was covered by screen. Inside the room was an antique chaise lounge. Well, that's what it had been. It was torn to pieces by the two raccoons that had inhabited the room for a week or so.

I have no idea where or how she would have got her hands on two raccoons and why she'd bring them in the house, but sure enough, there they were, frolicking around, shredding the chaise lounge, and pissing like two little fire hydrants.

Dad turned around and walked away. I followed him. We went downstairs where Peggy was waiting for us, arms folded under her bosom. "Did you find the leak?" she asked, looking very stern.

"Yes, I did," he replied, "but I don't have a packing to fit it."

Later that summer, we were "invited" back down because she said that all the packings in the house had to be replaced. "Are your faucets dripping?" my father asked her.

"It doesn't matter. They need replacing," she replied.
It's always best not to argue with a customer, especially Miss Peggy. The customer is always right. Just charge them plenty. Down we go, park the truck, and see Mrs. Hilliard for breakfast. About an hour later, tummies protruding, we're ready to go. I am about to start in on the first of god knows how many faucets when my dad came to me and said, "Miss Beckwith would like to see you." What? What the hell did I do? I agreed to eat three extra pancakes.

"Where is she?" I asked.

"She's upstairs … in her bedroom," Dad replied. I cannot tell you what was flying around my head. Suffice it to say that I was

[99]

slightly beyond nervous. I walked into her bedroom and saw another chaise lounge. This one was intact and did not smell like raccoon pee.

"Sit down," she said. My ears heard it more like a command. Down I sat.

"Do you know what a whale is?" I know I live in Vermont and we don't have an ocean, but it's not like I live in a cave.

"Yes, ma'am," I said politely.

"Have you ever HEARD a whale?" What the hell is this? Does she think I'm Lloyd Bridges or something? It's not like we have whales roaming out in the woods.

"No, ma'am," I said politely.

In front of me was an old Victrola record player, complete with the big "horn" and the large needle. A 33 1/3 album was on the flat, felt-covered disc. She placed the needle on the outer edge of the LP and what I heard is something I had most certainly never heard before. We didn't have YouTube back then. Clicks, whistles, moaning, groaning, weird outer-space-sounding noises. "What the hell is this?" I wondered to myself. No way would I ask.

"What do you think?" she asked.

"Different," I said. Twenty-two rather long minutes passed. The alien sounds ceased. I was anxious to get packing faucets.

 "Would you like to hear the other side?"

"Sure." Side two sounded remarkably like side one. I am still not sure whether or not she flipped the record over. Although I thought she was a little strange, I never thought her to be a cruel person. I'm sure she flipped it over. Years later I realized that in 1967 I was probably one of the only people in town who had ever

heard whales recorded. It takes a while for some things to sink in.
And to think I thought the Beatles were pretty cool!

Whose Country Is It, Anyway?

For those of you who have too much time on your hands and
choose to read this column regularly, you may recall in my last
column I mentioned how I had been engrossed in the HBO special;
"John Adams." That series wrapped up last week and much like
the feeling one gets when finishing a good book, I was sad to see it
over. Watching our history unfold with great imagery and camera
work was a great experience.

Thanks to this series I'm still somewhat fixated on the state of our
Union these days. We are seemingly on the threshold of perilous
times. Amazingly we are still stuck in Iraq (I wonder if another
columnist will be making this same statement a decade from now).
We are watching gas prices explode, catching up to the remarkable
rise in health care, food prices, and just about everything else.
The rise in gas prices has been somewhat amusing. Do you
remember back around Christmas when the news media were
telling us that gas prices were expected to reach $4.00 per gallon
this summer? Well, it's spring and we are now paying over
$3.50/gallon. It makes me wonder what's behind these kinds of
predictions. Is our government providing a service for oil
corporations by softening us up for price increases?

I've always been amused that when the cost of a barrel of oil goes
up, the price at the pump goes up the next day. However, if there
is a drop in the price of crude oil, it takes quite a while, if ever, for
the price to drop at the pumps. And what fun to learn that the oil
companies are recording record profits.

How does this happen in a country whose government is supposed
to be "Of the people, by the people and for the people"? Perhaps
the answer is that over the years the people are now playing a
subsidiary role to huge corporations. It could be the old "money
and politics" deal. If corporations are, as many believe, running

our country, then we should examine more closely what circumstances need to prevail for corporations to prosper.

Conflict. This is a good place to start. Where we have conflict we have opportunities. Iraq is a pretty good example. The war is costing Americans trillions of dollars racked up in debt. However, connected corporations like Halliburton and Blackwater have made off with billions of our tax dollars. The conflict in Iraq has led to fear and insecurities here at home and abroad. Home owners are losing their homes through sub-prime mortgages, yet there are hedge fund managers making billions at the expense of these poor souls.

Do WE need conflict? No. A friend of mine just returned from a trip to Israel. Like most people, I thought that Jews lived in Israel and Arabs in Palestine. From her I learned that Arabs and Jews live and work together in Israel. My friend seemed to think that life in Israel worked reasonably well. But what works for the people may not work for the government or other controlling groups. If Arabs and Jews can live peacefully together, then who would need Hamas? Like a manipulating corporation, Hamas needs the conflict that they continue to foster toward Israel. Arms corporations get to build and sell more weapons and build an industry around the conflict.

Conflict works well for corporate and political interests, but it does not work well for the average person. That is why when the average person has a conflict with a neighbor, they work hard to resolve the issues at hand. If resolution is elusive then we have the court system. We don't build an industry around the problem. The results are, for the most part, people are able to live in relative peace if left to their own devices.

So, how do we wrestle our nation away from corporate interests? It's not that hard, really. Get mad. Get involved. Run for office. Work on another's campaign. Stand up. Speak out. Write a letter to the papers.

[102]

Yeah, I know, you've heard this all before, right? After all, you are only one person. What can you do? Remember this—the Dali Lama is only one person. Hitler was only one person. The Pope is only one person. David Leser, CEO of Halliburton, is only one person.

All you need is one person. This nation is all about the individual. The only reason corporate interests have hijacked our government is because we, the individuals—you and I—have allowed it to happen. Our nation is built on a representative form of government. We elect from our peers a person to represent US. Once the money begins to flow from the corporations to the candidates, the focus of the representation changes. It is your job, our job, to ensure this doesn't happen and if it does, then we should damn well get mad and get busy to change it back to John Adams' vision of what our government was meant to be.

We're in the campaign season. What better time to begin?

April 27, 2008

Chapter 13

The Hills are Alive With the Sound of Music

Over the years I have found myself in some pretty odd situations as I'm sure you have, too. Ever wonder why?

We Are Where We're Supposed To Be

A friend said to me the other day: "We are where we're supposed to be." I oftentimes think that people say the strangest things. I don't know this happens to other people as well. These words caused me to ponder just what the heck my friend was talking about. I decided to let it go for the time being.

Today, 7-7-07, I went to the dump. We're supposed to call these places "transfer stations," but for me, once a dump always a dump. I'm recycling more than I'm throwing away, seeing old friends and chatting up a storm. Sure enough I run into a dear friend I've not seen in a while, we get to talking about our respective lives and how things are going.
The man who runs the dump, er, transfer station (we'll call him "Dick" since that's his name) comes on the scene and in no time the three of us are going on about this, that, and the other. We're talking about our kids and the fact that my daughter, Meredith, is about to be married in less than a month.

It wasn't long before the discussion of the wedding veered off to a discussion about money and that we never seem to have enough of it. Dick and I both agreed that winning the lottery would make all the difference. "Why would you want to ruin an otherwise great life?" my friend asked. Now there was a showstopper of a question.

I think that we have all pondered the idea of being richer than we currently are at one time or another. If you haven't yet done so, might I respectfully suggest that you try it. It's great for your imagination to run amuck as you think about what you would do, where you would go, how differently things might be.

"Ruin an otherwise good life, eh?" That one line sent me off into a train of thought as I was mowing my way-too-big lawn. I realized how we do tend to think about the "what-ifs" or the "coulda, woulda, shoulda" things we might have done with our lives. Comes with getting older, I guess.

Gee, if only I had the money to do ____ (fill in the blank). My friend suggested that perhaps instead of ciphering on what we "might" have, maybe we'd all be better off if we examined and appreciated what we "do" have. Wow, there's a concept.

I started thinking about where I am and what I do have and did a little research on where I fit in with the rest of the world. Think about this for a second. If we could consolidate the world's population down to one village of only 100 people, the following is a breakdown of what that village would look like:

There would be 57 Asians; 21 Europeans, 14 from the Western Hemisphere, 8 Africans; 52 would be female, 48 male; 70 would be non-white, 30 would be white; 70 would be non-Christian, 30 would be Christian; 89 would be heterosexual, 11 would be homosexual; 6 would posses 59 percent of the wealth (all representing the U.S.); 80 would be living in substandard housing; 70 would be unable to read.
Half of the village would suffer from malnutrition. One would be near death; one would be ready to give birth. Only one would have a college education and only one would own a computer.

If you woke up this morning in good health, you are ahead of the one million people who will not survive the week. If you have never experienced battle, been imprisoned or tortured or suffered starvation, you are ahead of 500 million people who have. If you have food in your refrigerator, clothing and shelter, you are richer than 75 percent of the people with whom you share the world.

If you have any money in the bank or your wallet, you are among the top 8 percent of the world's wealthiest people. If you can read this column, you are ahead of the 2 billion who cannot.

[106]

Sometimes we need a trip to the dump and to see old friends to understand just how well off we are. Maybe we are where we're supposed to be. I can't say for sure. But I can say that compared to many in this world, you and I are in an OK place.

July 7, 2007

It's about timing. Step off the curb at the wrong split second and you're a blotch on the road that can be removed only after numerous rain showers. Hold off just a second and whoosh— you're across the street unscathed.

As a musician for 40 years, I have developed a keen sense of timing. Music helps you learn to live in the moment. Catch the groove. Feel the beat. Everything I ever learned from music can be applied to everyday life.

You may not know it, but many Vermonters play some kind of musical instrument. You may not recognize it as such, but music plays a prominent role. When you are in a recession and don't have a lot of money, or a prayer of ever getting any, you have to be creative. Once you're done building your house, you can always use your saw to make music. The same does not apply, generally speaking, to your hammer. Learn to play an instrument. You don't have to be good, just enthusiastic.

Being at the right place at the right time makes all the difference. Remember, you are where you're supposed to be. This all relates to how to live in Vermont, which in turn helps prepare you to survive a recession. First, it's helpful to be incredibly lucky. Sure, talent is helpful, but it doesn't hold a candle to luck. There are hundreds of thousands of great musicians in this country. Unfortunately, there is only a handful that you get to meet through venues like American Idol. These chosen few are just the tip of the talent iceberg. Vermont alone has some of the most accomplished musicians in the world. Guys like Paul Aspel, Dennis Willmott,

Chris Kleeman, Tom Buckley, Jason Corbiere, Nick Sherman, Billy "Silvertone" Carruth, Jimmy Branca, Rick Redington, Duane Carleton, Steve Thurston, Laura Molinelli, and Banjo Dan come to mind. I've played with most of these folks.

I've also had the privilege of playing with or opening for a few out-of-staters, too. BB King, Charlie Musselwhite, John Hammond, Jonathan Edwards, Sarah Leigh Guthrie and Johnny Irions, Mark Hummel, Lynard Skynard, Buddy Guy, Joe Sample, Issac Hayes, Stephen King (the writer), David Maxwell, Louisiana Red, David "Honey Boy" Edwards, and other great players.

Each one comes with a story, but how I stumbled upon meeting BB King is an interesting tale. It started where most things began for me—mowing lawns.

Back in the '70s, one of my customers was Barbara Riley Levin and Jerry Levin. He was the guy who ended up being CEO of AOL-Time/Warner. They bought a little place here in Vermont in what was once an old orchard and hired me to mow their lawn. I sold the business in '82 and that was the last time I saw them. Two decades passed and Alison and I coincidentally (if you happen to be one of those who believes in coincidences; I don't) ran into Barbara three times in one week.

Beautiful thing about Vermont. You may not see someone for 20 years, yet the state is so small that you then see that someone three times in one week. After the third chance encounter, Barbara invited us over for cocktails. "What are you doing Saturday night?" Before I could answer the question she said, "Cancel it. You're coming to our place for cocktails." Silly her. Like we would have plans.

We arrived at their place to find that we had to park a quarter mile away. Some cocktail party. Turns out it was a party for the staff of the Riley Rink, a local indoor-outdoor concert site. Tom Perini, a Texas BBQ caterer, was brought in to do the food and Margaritas. Clint Bullard and his band came in from Nashville.

[108]

I never go to a party without a few harps in my pockets (could never have done this with my drums). You never know when you might be asked to play. Oh, for those of you who think I am referring to a harp as in "with strings," I like to tell people not in this life or any other life will I be playing one of those. I'm talking about the harmonica.

Alison wanted to dance so off to the dance floor we went. Within seconds I noticed an old friend and former employee of mine in my old lawn business, Brad Tyler (son of Terry), up near the stage talking to Barbara. I knew just what he was doing, so I asked Alison to dance merrily for a minute and I went up to join them.

"What are you doing, Typecker," (his affectionate nickname).

"Those are my drums up there. I'm loaning them to the drummer in exchange for a chance to play them with this band."

"Sweet. You're not going up there without me," I said, which caused a big smile to appear on Brad's face.

"What do you play?" Barbara queried.

"Harmonica."

Barbara grabbed the star, Bullard, and said, "I want this guy to play drums and this guy to play the harmonica."

Clint looked mildly uncomfortable, as most guitarists look when they hear those frightening words, "I'm a harmonica player; can I sit in?" We walked up on the stage and Clint said, "What do you want to play?"

"I'm a Blues player."

"I don't do that shit," he said and walked off the stage. Ouch.

[109]

The guitarist, who had been on the road for the past year with Faith Hill, grinned and said, "A Blues player, eh?" I gave the band a quick four count and off we went. We played hard and fast for about 10 minutes. Barbara and Jerry were right in front of the stage, looking like they were enjoying what they were hearing.

I played. The audience clapped. I had another Margarita. Life was good. The next day I got a call from Bill Daiek, a man who worked for Barbara. "Barbara wants to know if you have a band and if you would be willing to play at the VIP dinner for the sponsors of the BB King show coming up in three weeks."

"Sure, that would be great. Book it."

I had no band. But I did know Chris Kleeman, whom I called immediately. "I don't have a band right now but I can pull one together in three weeks." The bass player and drummer met at the gig. No rehearsal or set list. Just a ton of stress.

The gig was at Equinox Pond in Manchester at the Pavilion Building. About 75 people were in attendance. We did a set. No one got hurt. During the break Daiek approached me. "Barbara has a friend here who plays harmonica. Would you mind if he sits in for a song or two?" I'm one of those musicians who has always been agreeable to letting quality players join us on stage. Plus, I was getting paid $100 bucks. What did I care?

A serious man older than I approached the stage. The band started playing and so did he. He was great. After a couple of songs he said, "Do you like this band?" and of course the audience politely applauded, bless their hearts. "Good, so do I. You will get to hear them next year in Montreux."

Hearing loss is a horrible tragedy and has been responsible for more than one embarrassing moment. Fortunately, as a born and raised Vermonter I have been well trained to handle embarrassing situations.

[110]

I was off on the side of the stage when this invite was made. I was pretty sure that the small man with white hair and an accent, sounded French to me, but all accents with the exception of those folks from Maine, all sound like French to most Vermonters, had invited us to "Montreal." I walked right up to Daiek and said, "Hey, dig that. Looks like I'm going to Montreal."

"Why?" he asked.

"Well, the white-haired dude just invited us."

"You moron. That's Claude Nobs; the founder of the Montreux Jazz Festival. You're going to Switzerland."

"Oh, yeah, right. I knew that."

I was numb. The Montreux Jazz Festival is the most prestigious festival in the world. Was this really happening? Before the impact of this offer had a chance to set in, we were approached by this very happy man wearing the most awesome red and white leather baseball jacket I've ever seen. Across the back of the jacket read, "BB KING WORLD TOUR 2000." This guy looked like somebody. Nobody from Vermont, but nevertheless, somebody.

"Hi, my name is Floyd Lieberman. I am BB King's manager. Would you guys be willing to come to New York and play BB's club?" Once again I had that feeling that I was in a movie or a dream.

"Well, we can't come down in July because we'll be in Switzerland, but some other time might work." (It's always valuable to let someone trying to book you for a show know that you are very, very busy.)

"Here's my card. Get in touch. I want you guys to play at the second anniversary of his club in Times Square."

[111]

Knock me over with a flea fart. I'm down to words like, "er" and "um" and "gahgggerum" when Claude Nobs returned to the stage. "Could I ask you and the guitarist to do me a favor?" Oh yeah. Here we go. Get invited to Switzerland and now he probably needs a right arm from a Vermonter to add to his collection of right arms that he's secured over the years.

"Sure. What's up?"

"Would the two of you be willing to join BB King on stage for a jam session after his show tomorrow night?"

Breathing slowly in through my nose and out through my mouth I replied, "Man, I don't know. I have great third row seats, which I hate to give up." To be a successful rock star one should oftentimes play hard to get, but not for long. "OK, sure. That'd be great!"

We arrived at the Riley Rink the next day. It was an all day Blues show with BB King as the headliner. Chris and I opened the show. The day passed by slowly. We did our thing. Other bands did their thing. BB did his thing. While he was on stage we were told to be on the ready. Our charge was to walk on the stage while BB was playing and sit in the seats that were set up there. Sounds easy enough, doesn't it?

You wish. As we're waiting to go on, Chris decided that he wanted to go out to his car and get another amp. I told him to hurry as we were going on any minute. He had not yet returned when a very large black man in a gold suit with a gold fedora and gold everything else except his black sunglasses said, "OK, time to go on."

"My guitarist is not back yet," I said.

"I don't give a shit. Your job is to walk out there, sit down, and start playing." Music is not always fun and games. Chris made it back just as we were walking on stage.

At this point I assumed I had all of my harps in a leather fanny pouch. I'm listening to the song BB was playing while sitting with his back to us. I'm pulling harps out of the pouch and playing them to see which one I need. At the time I was a good second position harp player, but not a great first position player. (To learn more about harp playing call me and set up a session. Note, however, that it will cost you a lot more than this book did.) I looked at Harry Ralph, an amazing fiddle player who was going to join us. "What key is he in?" I asked.

"B-flat," he replied. That would mean that I needed an E-flat harp, which I did not have.

The feeling that washed over me was similar to that of bringing a knife to a gun fight. Here I was, 50 years old, on stage in front of 4,000 people and playing with BB King for the first time—and I didn't have the right harmonica! "Suck it up," I thought to myself. I grabbed the B-flat harp and played in first position. For the record, today I am a much better first position player. Fear is a great motivator and if you live in Vermont, you learn a lot about fear (reread the card game).

I sat down right next to BB on his right. We're playing this slow Blues tune and I'm picking out single high notes, wondering to myself whether or not BB would notice if I crap my pants. One more thing to worry about.

Things were going OK when suddenly BB turned and looked right at me. "After this next solo we're going to pick up the pace a little bit." These were not welcome words. They ranked right up there with "we are now going to proceed with the water boarding, Mr. Stannard."

Nervously, I looked into the eyes of a man who's seen it all. I said, "I wouldn't mind if you changed keys while we're at it." BB King has the most expressive face of any man I've ever met. His brow furrowed. A scowl came across his face that would have made a weaker man just die right there on the spot.

"And what key would you like to play in, sir?"

Oh man. I AM going to die. "Anything but "Bb." I don't have an "Eb" harp on me." The scowl melted away and his trademark smile, the one that makes everyone around him feel like a million bucks, appeared.

"Well, you've been doing a mighty fine job of fakin' it." He turned his head a little further to the right and hollering out to no one in particular shouted out, "Pick it up in "G," boys," and off we went. You will recall that the "C" Marine Band was my first harp. It is the harp you use when the band is playing in the key of "G." I was in heaven.

That following summer, Chris Kleeman and I brought the band to New York City to open for BB for the second anniversary of his club in Times Square. We did four nights with him. I had never played anywhere in New York City. After playing at BB King's where else do you go?

The author swapping chops with Montreux Jazz Festival founder, Claude Nobs.
Photo: Lee Krohn

BB King & Howlin' Wolf

It was the night of Monday, June 24, 2002. BB King had just
finished his last of four shows at the second anniversary of his club
in Times Square, New York City. Chris Kleeman and I had asked
for a brief audience with BB so that we could thank him for the
incredible honor of opening for him each night.

We had preferred to meet with BB prior to his last show so that we
might avoid the onslaught of people who wish to see him every
night. Unfortunately, that wasn't to be, so we were caught up in
the herd.

When we finally got the nod from Floyd Lieberman, BB's manager
and, incidentally, one great person, we trotted right on in with
Chris's family and a couple of other people. We thanked BB and
told him what a thrill and honor it had been to be with him these
last few days and then spent a few minutes just chillin'.

Finally, Floyd looked at his watch and gave us the "high sign." I
rose up from my chair and shook BB's hand one last time. BB
looked right into my eyes and said, "You in some sorta hurry,
son?" I looked at Floyd, who shrugged his shoulders and gave me
that "don't look at me" look, and said, "Why no, BB," and sat right
back down.

BB leaned forward and said, "I thought I might tell you boys about
a time before I was ever known as BB, I was just Riley King. I
was invited to play with a guy named Howlin' Wolf." BB looked
at Chris and me and said, "You boys ever hear of Howlin' Wolf?"

"Why yes, of course. We've been listening to and playing his stuff
for years," Chris said.

"Well, Howlin' Wolf was playing at a juke joint in Mississippi
owned by a man named Willy Ford. He'd been there for a while,
we met and he invited me to sit in with him," BB said.

[115]

"There came a time when Howlin' had to go away for a couple of weeks and asked that I take over for him while he's away. I was excited to say the least." BB looked at me and said, "At this time in my life, I had quite a way with the ladies and for the two weeks I was at the club I, shall we say, worked the crowd. I was playing well and getting along good with the audience (especially the ladies) when sure enough, Howlin' Wolf returned. Willy Ford called us into the office to tell us that we were both good players, but that he could only afford one of us," he said.

"Willy Ford said, 'I can't make this decision on my own. I'm gonna let the audience decide tonight when you both will be playing on stage.' I thought to myself that I had a pretty good 'in' with the crowd," BB said as he winked at both of us.

"Later that night we were both on stage and Howlin' Wolf would play and Willy Ford stood behind him with his hand over his head and the audience applauded. Then it was my turn and Willy put his hand over my head and the audience applauded just a little louder. Of course, I was lookin' at some of the pretty ladies in the audience," said BB.

"Willy Ford said, 'That was pretty close, so now we're gonna have you both sing.' " BB looked at Chris and me and said in a very low, solemn voice, "Have you boys ever heard Howlin' Wolf sing?" Mesmerized, Chris and I nodded our heads. "Nobody on God's green earth has ever sung like Howlin' Wolf and I don't expect they ever will," said BB. "Howlin' Wolf began to sing … and Riley King began to cry."

And that's the story of Riley "BB" King getting beat out of a gig at Willy Ford's club in Mississippi. Although BB never said how old he was, I can only guess that he must have been around 17 to 19 years old. What an evening.

[116]

The author, BB King & Chris Kleeman
Photo: George Kalinsky

BB King - The Bus

Some days work out easier than others. Yesterday I opened for BB
King at Riley Rink in my hometown of Manchester. This should
have been a great event with easy access backstage. After all, I
spent 3 days backstage at the Montreux Jazz Festival being treated
like a king the entire time.

I was scheduled to play with the Chris Kleeman Band from 4:00
to 4:30 opening the BB King Blues Festival. We opened for Shane
Henry, The Fabulous Thunderbirds, and Susan Tedschi. Pretty
good lineup. We were told before we went on that as soon as we
were done playing, we would no longer have any access
backstage! So much for being rock stars. This was certainly going
to interfere with our plans to get the bottle of nice wine that we
promised Caleb Emphrey, BB's drummer, when we were together
in Montreux. We told him that when he came to Manchester, we'd
treat him right.

I had previously arranged through Lieberman Management to get
backstage and on the bus with BB either before or after the show. I

[117]

was hoping to thank BB King for this past incredible year on this one-year anniversary, but things were not looking up

Things were looking pretty bleak. I had no access. My contacts were nowhere to be found.

I was standing out by the lawn when I felt a hand on my shoulder. Martial arts training caused me to relax and defensively turn around only to see the round, black smiling face of Greg, one of BB's security staff. He said to meet him by the side entrance and he'd get us backstage. I rounded up Chris and we waited for him to show up. Good news and bad news. Greg was able to get only one "All Access" pass. In a moment of sincere graciousness, Chris said, "This is your gig, you take it." Greg said, "You didn't get this from me," and I said not to worry. I grabbed Chris's backpack with the wine and headed off.

Backstage I got to say hello to band members Stanley Abernathy, Walter King, and Melvin Jackson. One of BB's road staff, Nasty Norman, was also on hand, but from experience I've learned that he's not one you say hello to, hence the nickname. I walked further back into the room and still no Caleb. Suddenly he appeared from behind the curtain, looked at me and said, "Is there something in that bag for me?" He smiled and gave me a hug. I told him that he had his choice of either bottle. He grabbed the first one he saw and was grateful. He asked where Chris was and I said that I was able to get only one pass. He was not happy. He went into the back room and immediately returned with a second pass.

This really was like pulling teeth. I was stopped by security and asked where I got the All Access Pass. I pointed to Caleb and said, "That guy right over there, BB's drummer, gave me these." That was the end of that. As BB's show came to a close, Bill Daiek, a true candidate for sainthood, was handing out backstage passes to the VIP sponsors. He came over to me and gave me four passes for Mom, Dick, Alison, and myself. Alison gave her pass to Mary McFall. We rolled my Mom backstage and waited for the big man

[118]

to make an appearance. Unfortunately, BB went straight to the bus and never did come backstage.

I tried to get past Rocky who works at the Rink, but he would have none of it. Nobody was going back to the bus. I couldn't believe this. I know BB was expecting us, because it had been set up, but the fortress was built and there was no getting through.

Just about the time Chris and I decided to bag it, BB's grandson, Kevin, came walking by. We'd come to know him pretty well through our contact over the past year. I asked him to take us back to the bus. He turned right around and led us past the "pitbulls" and right to the bus. *To* the bus, not *on* the bus. Kevin went on the bus and was scoping the scene. The Levins and Claude Nobs, the founder and CEO of the Montreux Jazz Festival, were on the bus along with another couple, Claude's friend Tony and photographer Lee Krohn.

We saw Tina, our contact from Lieberman, as she was leaving and I hollered over to her. She said just ask Sherman Darby about getting on the bus. My heart sank. Sherman can be a nice guy, actually, he is a gentleman, but he has an edge, for sure. In a gruff voice Sherman told us that all of those who were invited on the bus had already been on the bus and that they were winding down. So close, yet so far.

We could see Bill Daiek sitting on the couch. He got up, came down the steps, and said that they were just about done and that we could quickly just say hello. FINALLY!!! Chris boarded first and I followed. We walked past the security and down the narrow corridor to BB's room. Barbara was sitting to BB's right. On her right was a young couple. On their right was Jerry and to his right was Tony, Claude's friend. Claude was sitting across the little desk from BB.

Chris entered the room and BB said, "Hello there" with a big smile of recognition on his face. I poked my head in the room and he smiled and said, "Well, well, look who you have with you. We

[119]

meet in the darndest places!" I pulled open the lapels of my suit jacket and exposed the Montreux Jazz Festival T-shirt that I had been wearing and said, "Long time no see."

After the intros, BB started telling a story as only he can tell it. He talked about his former manager, Sid Sidenberg, and how he had been so instrumental in advancing his career. He spoke admirably about Sid's replacement, Floyd Lieberman (my new best friend), and compared this new relationship to a second marriage. He looked at Barbara, smiled, and said, "And that's something I know a little about." Although the dynamics with his managerial staff had changed, it was easy to tell he was happy and comfortable with the way his business affairs were being managed.

Like sliding into an old pair of sneakers, BB turned the conversation to his life and how, now that he's older, he sees things differently. He announced that now, every day is a special and wonderful day. "I have begun thinking about the time when I will leave this planet. I started thinking about it about 10 or 15 years ago, but as more time goes by, leaving becomes more a part of my thoughts. Of course, this makes Floyd very nervous," he said with a hearty chuckle. "Little things that at one time had no importance, because I was in a hurry going here and there and doing this and that, I now pay more attention to. I stop to think of all the friends I have all over the world and realize how blessed I am," he said.

BB talked of the gift of friendship that he has received from so many. He looked right up at me with his beautiful face and piercing yet sincere eyes and said, "And you have given me one of my greatest gifts by playing with me at Montreux." I almost cried. I looked over my shoulder at Chris, knowing his words were directed to us both. There is probably no other person on this earth who can make you feel so good about yourself or about life than BB King. He has a way about him that makes the people around him feel very special. What a gift.

He talked a little bit about his first manager. Claude brought this man up, saying that he had exploited BB and taken much of his

[120]

money. BB smiled and said, "Yeeaaahh, but I really did like the man." Holding no ill feelings at having been stripped of his claim to many of his early songs and much of his money (as was the case with most black musicians of his day), he went on: "When I was younger and we'd be in Vegas, I'd spend my money on gamblin' and drinkin' and women and I'd have no mo' money. I would go to him and say, 'I have no mo' money,' and he would dig in his pocket and say, 'I only have $40,' and hand it right over." With genuine admiration he surveyed the room and said, "That's what I call a true a friend." I can only guess how many thousands of dollars this guy bilked BB out of, but there was definitely no malice in BB's eyes. If he ever felt that he had been taken advantage of, you couldn't prove it by the words he spoke that evening.

During this story he mentioned that he had been a disc jockey and how he liked Bing Crosby's version of "Mule Train" better than the original artist. Whenever he would play this song, he played Crosby's version. It was very cool to watch, as BB would mention the name of a song, yet struggle to remember the artist (kinda like I'm doing here), only to have Jerry Levin pull the name right out of his old musical artists mental database. Barbara suggested that he see about getting on the game show "Jeopardy." BB just chuckled and shook as he did so. And on this light note we bid the King of the Blues *adieu.*

Before we left, BB asked Chris and me if we'd be getting together any time soon. I said that Floyd had offered us a show with him at his club at the Foxwood Casino in Connecticut. His eyes lit right up and he said that he would look forward to seeing us then. We all agreed it would be good to be together again.

It'll be a while before I come down from all of this!

Another Evening with BB King

Thanks to BB King's manager, Floyd Lieberman of Lieberman Management, on January 17 and 18, 2003, I was given the opportunity to play at the one-year anniversary of the BB King Nite Club at the Foxwoods Casino in Mashantucket, Connecticut. Joining me was Chris Kleeman on guitar, Marcus Copening on drums, and Mike Byrd on bass.

The trip down was more stressful than it needed to be. I was about 45 miles from home when I realized I had forgotten all of my clothes for the weekend. I had to turn around, drive back home, get my clothes, and then drive back to Brattleboro, Vermont, and on down to Foxwoods. Of course, I had no directions because I had planned to carpool with Chris, so he had to guide me in via cell phone. My cell phone bill was about as much as my mortgage payment that month.

We played the BB King Nite Club on that Friday night and did pretty well. Floyd and his family and friends stopped by for our last set and seemed to enjoy themselves. There were rumors that maybe BB would join us for a song or two, but it didn't happen. Floyd suggested that it might happen the following night, but it wasn't meant to be.

Were we disappointed? Sure, of course. But I have come to learn that in the music business you take what you get. If great things happens, all the better. If not, it's not the end of the world.

What did happen, however, was that we were given another opportunity to meet with BB King in his dressing room before the show; something that rarely happens. We were told we only had a few minutes. It lasted an hour. And what a great hour it was.

When I reached the age of 50 (June 16, 2001) I realized that we all have only one true asset—our time. How it is invested is up to each individual. BB King is incredibly generous with his time and gives it away freely. Many a celebrity would be happy just to sign your memorabilia and send you on your merry way. BB King seems happiest when he invites you to sit right down and jaw a while. This willingness to make you feel like his best friend defines his character.

Chris, Marcus, Mike, and I were escorted into his dressing room at about 8:05 p.m. We were to go on at 9:00 p.m. I assumed we would have about 10 minutes to visit. We were all introduced to the various people in the room, one of whom was Tom Cantone, V.P. of Entertainment for Foxwoods. Tom once held the same position at the Sands Hotel in Las Vegas. As we shook hands Tom said, "I've heard a lot of good things about you from Floyd." I looked over at Floyd, who was sitting on the sofa with Tom. He just smiled and winked. I smiled right back at him.

I sat down; Chris and the boys remained standing. Naturally, I removed my hat when I entered the room. After the pleasantries, BB looked at me and said, "Bob, I am about to make an observation and I hope that you will not be offended."

I looked at BB and said, "BB, I sincerely doubt that you would ever offend me or anyone, so please, by all means proceed."

He said, "I would like to make an observation about your hair." (I am quite bald. I shave my head.) I smiled. He asked, "Do you know why some men lose their hair?"

I said that I had my theories, but would like to hear his thoughts on the matter.

"Brains," he said. "Do you understand what I'm saying? It's big brains. A man's brain is so big that it's just pushin' the hair right off his head."

The room became very quiet and some felt a bit uncomfortable. That was until BB removed his hat and pointed to his own, thinning hair and said, "Now you can see that my wavy hair of the past has begun to thin quite a bit. Yes, it's taken a lifetime for my own brain to finally mature!" I smiled. The room breathed a sigh of relief. Few people can make you feel more at ease than BB King.

[123]

Our allotted 10 minutes flew by. I looked up to see that Floyd was adjusting his wrist for a better view of his watch. I didn't need to have it in writing. I stood and said to BB that it was a pleasure to be in his company once again and extended my hand.

He scowled and said, "Are you in some sort of hurry, Bob?" I looked over at Floyd, who now found something very interesting to look at over his right shoulder. The moment became an awkward one. "Why don't you just have a seat?" said BB. Not sure whether the smart money here was to appease Floyd or BB, I opted to go with The King.

After getting comfortable (again), Floyd mentioned that BB was about to embark on writing his autobiography. I said that this was a marvelous idea and that I hoped he would include his story about him and Howlin' Wolf at Willy Ford Juke Joint in Mississippi. BB's eyes shifted toward me and he said, "You remember the name of the man who owned the juke joint, Willy Ford?" I said, "Of course. I remember every word of that story you told me." My comments were rewarded with a great big smile and he said, "Well tell me if this is the right story," and proceeded to tell the following:

It turned out that BB was opening for Howlin' Wolf at Willy Ford's club and at the end of his performance, the crowd was really hootin' and hollarin'. He could tell that the people really liked his show. He was backstage with his band listening to Howlin' Wolf play and after about 15 minutes or so the crowd was really getting worked up. "The girls were all screaming and yelling; much more so then when I played." he said. "I told my bass player, 'Let's go see what all the fuss is about,' and we went out into the audience. There was Howlin' Wolf on stage on his knees and lying right over backwards, singing and playing like only he could. However, little did Wolf know that the seam in his pants had let go and his underwear wasn't holdin' nothin' back! I don't think I can ever top that!" BB said.

BB turned his head in my direction and asked, "Was that the same story?" I said, "No BB. I was referring to the story of Howlin' Wolf beating you out of the gig at Willy Ford's club." "Oh, *that* story," he said and proceeded to retell the story he'd told me in New York nearly word for word. When he was done and everyone was in the room was as amazed at hearing it as I had been when I heard it the first time. He looked at me and asked, "Is that it?" "Yep, that's the one." I said. BB rocked back in his chair, gave the room a big smile that just about made you melt, and said, "You can tell when I tell a true story and I ain't lying when I tell the same story the same way twice." The room erupted into laughter.

He went on talking about getting to his life as a performer. Floyd pointed out that BB King has never missed a gig in 52 years. If you are a touring musician reading this, you understand just how incredible a feat this is. "We were almost late for a few, weren't we Floyd?" he bellowed to his manager. Floyd told of one gig where they had to get right off the plane, into a car, drive like crazy to get to the gig, and had no time to do anything but grab Lucille, BB's guitar, and begin playing.

BB then told of a time when they were delayed in North Africa, when a president of one of the countries over there was going to be on the same plane. "You will have to sit in the back of the plane and you won't be able to go near the side of the plane where the president will be sitting," BB was told.

"That's not the first time I was told to get myself to the back," he said. It was hard for me to think that there was ever a time that this great and generous man would have been treated like a second-class citizen, as were all black people of his generation, but here I was hearing it live from the man.

Marcus, who is African American, said, "So there really was once a time when you were not THE king?"

BB said, "Oh yeah. On that plane, I was just Riley."

[125]

It was now a few minutes before 9:00 p.m. and we had to go on. I looked at BB and said, "Well BB, we have to go to work."

He glared at me with his piercing eyes and said, "I'm very glad to hear you refer to what we do as work, Bob. Many musicians will say that they have to go play, but it really is work and I'm glad you see it as such."

I replied, "I have always felt that if someone is paying me to do something, then it is work and should be viewed that way. Just because I'm having fun doesn't mean it's not work."

He pointed to Tom Cantone, sitting on the couch wearing his red and white leather baseball jacket, with not one hair out of place and said, "See that man? He is my boss."

Tom, now feeling slightly uncomfortable at having been singled out, replied, "BB, I'm not your boss. Nobody's your boss."

"You are the one paying me for tonight and that makes you my boss," BB said with great laughter. We all stood up, shook hands, and sped off to our awaiting audience.

There is one more observation that I would like to make. When I walked into the BB King Nite Club, the first thing I noticed was an old poster of a much younger BB King sitting on a bench. On his left was a young man holding his guitar. He was about the same age as my son, Wesley, is now; about twenty. This young boy was Eric Clapton.

I stared at this poster and thought to myself how he must have felt sitting next to BB King and trading a few chops. By this time I had played with BB twice—once in Manchester, Vermont, and then again at the Montreux Jazz Festival in Switzerland in a jam session with BB & Joe Sample. It was a strange feeling to look at this poster and know that Clapton and I at one point in our lives shared the same extraordinary feeling that you can only get sitting next to and playing with the King of the Blues: BB King.

Chapter 14

More Life Lessons Through Music

Now that we're going down this music path, perhaps this would be a good time to remind you, once again, of the importance of being poor. Well, maybe not poor, per se, but shall we say, down pretty near the bottom of the "we're-so-rich-that-darn-little-bothers-us-much" pile.

Being poor provides you with the necessary skills for things like recessions and depressions. To quote Bobby Dylan, "When you got nothing, you got nothing to lose." So, as you can see, by being poor you are already one step ahead of everyone else.

For the most part, musicians are a poor lot. Sure, some of them have scraped and groveled their way up the food chain, but for the most part, the side of the road is littered with starving musicians.

Of the ones who have done OK, John Hammond stands out. John is one of those unique players who, after being told by his relatively famous father of the same name NOT to go into the music business, left home at the age of about 20 to go into the music business. Not listening to one's parents, or any adults for that matter, is also a trait common in successful musicians. There has never been a parent anywhere on the planet who said to their little Johnny or Janis, "Honey, when you grow up I want you to go right out on the road and become a musician." Most parents would rather you be a cowboy and there are darn few who would encourage that as a career.

It was January of 2003. I got a call from Chris Kleeman, a great guitarist and vocalist with whom I did my first album, "Made in Vermont: LIVE Performances from Obscure but Popular Places." We couldn't think of a longer title.

The author sharing the stage with Country Blues legend, John Hammond

Chris informed me that he was opening for John Hammond at the Iron Horse Café in Northampton, Massachusetts, and asked if I wanted in the on the gig. "I can't guarantee that you'll play, man, because I haven't cleared it with anyone, but what the hell. Bring your gear and if it works, it works. If not, you get to see John Hammond. It's a win-win either way for you."

Never having been one for looking a gift horse in the mouth (or anywhere else for that matter), I grabbed an amp, my harps, and whatever else I thought I'd need, met up with Chris in Brattleboro, Vermont, and off we went. Of course, it was snowing and cold. When we arrived at the Iron Horse, Chris immediately went searching for the manager, who was nowhere to be found.

"Screw it," he said. "Let's just go to the green room and see if John is there." We went downstairs and walked over to the closed door. Chris had played this venue before and knew right where he was going. He knocked on the door. It opened and there stood John Hammond. He's a tall one—6'3" at least, maybe more. His thick white hair was combed back. He's a very handsome man.

Chris said hello and introduced me. "Bob plays harmonica and I'd like to have him open the show with me, but I'm not sure how you'd feel about a duo opening for you as a solo act."

John Hammond put his arm around my shoulders and said, "Hey, this guy came all the way down here to play; we can't not have him play."

Talk about makin' you feel like a million bucks. Here I was thoroughly expecting to get rejected, only to have this guy whom I have listened to and admired for over 30 years make me feel great. "Come on in and say hello to Marla." Marla is John's wife; a real hot ticket. She's as sweet as she can be, yet can be real tough when the situation calls for it. Word to the wise: don't mess with Marla. Not one for ever wanting to mess with anyone, Marla and I became friends right off.

"Hey, Marla," John said. "Check out the jacket this guy is wearing." I was wearing an Orvis mid-length, leather coat that was quilt lined. Orvis had bought out a company known as Gokie—a world-famous leather company. I got the coat at an Orvis tent sale. It had been returned. Someone who could afford to spend $700 had purchased it new and used it quite a while before the zipper lost a tooth and he returned it. Companies like Orvis will take stuff back no questions asked. Never in a million years would the previous owner of this fine jacket (minus the missing tooth in the zipper, which ironically did not prohibit one from zipping up the coat) have a clue of the good fortune that was about to come the way of its new owner.

"Take a look at my coat over there, Bob," John said. Draped over a chair was the exact same coat I was wearing, only his was a Gokie coat. "I got that coat twenty-five years ago. I wear it every winter. I love that coat."

"Where'd you say you were from?" he asked.

[131]

"Manchester, Vermont," I replied. John smiled and looked at Marla, who was also smiling. Why was everyone smiling? There was something going on.

"Marla, what's the name of that place we stay when we go on vacation?" Marla pulled out her little notebook that had the names of all the places they stay and of all of their friends.

"The Weathervane Motel," she said.

It's nearly an icon in Manchester—been there forever. "You guys stay at the Weathervane Motel?"

"Yeah, we don't get much vacation time, but when we do, we like to go up to Manchester and stay there. There is a great backyard at that place." Who knew?

Chris and John got into a rap about guitars. John plays a 1939 National Steel guitar. Chris has the same guitar but his is a 1937. John offers to swap. Chris doesn't accept the offer. John mentioned that the old Nationals were made before they had guitar straps and were made to be able to stand up on their own. Chris had no idea about this. John said, "Yeah, check this out," and stood up his guitar. The neck was at about 10:00. "Well I'll be darned," said Chris and he stood up his guitar as well, which was at about 2:00. I said, "How 'bout you two guys leaning forward a little bit," and I snapped a great photograph of the two of them with their guitars standing up big as you please.

"OK," I said. "Enough of this guitar talk. I'm a harmonica player. Feel like playing something?" Instead of being escorted out of the green room, John picked up his guitar. Chris picked up his and we began to play. The three of us played for about half an hour while Marla worked on her crossword puzzle. Four people in a dingy little green room having more fun than we should have been allowed to have.

The time flew by and it was now time for us to go open the show. About halfway through our set, I looked at the packed house and asked, "You folks like what you're hearing up here?" The place erupted with applause (something a musician never tires of hearing). "That's great because the man coming out here after us is going to do the same stuff all by himself." The house went wild.

We wrapped up our set and as we left the stage, John and I passed at the top of the stairs. "You're a mighty fine harp player, man." He didn't have to say that. He could've just gone up and done his show. There are people in the world who transcend wealth and fame. They are just good human beings, because that's what they choose to be. There are few people I have ever met who are as kind, thoughtful, talented, and just plain good as John Hammond.

Almost a year later, I was sitting in my office when my phone rang. The caller ID said HAMMOND. "What? Who is this," I thought to myself.

"Hi, Bob. This is John Hammond. I don't know if you remember me. We met at the Iron Horse a while back. I'm playing up your way and wanted to know if you and your wife wanted be my guests."

"DON'T KNOW IF I REMEMBER YOU!" I screamed to myself in my head. "Yeah, sure I remember you," I said. As fate would have it, we couldn't make the show because we were hosting a birthday party for my best friend. ("Hey, Alison. We don't really have to be at the house. They can have the party without us being there, can't they?"
Nothing doing.)

"Well, that's OK. It was short notice. You available for lunch tomorrow?" he asked. Jumpin'-sweet-Jesus am I the luckiest man alive or what? "Sure."

The following is an account of the second meeting with John and Marla Hammond.

[133]

December 6, 2004

I'm working away in my office on this particular afternoon, when at 2:30 p.m. the phone rings. The following is the conversation:

J.H.: Hi Bob, this is John Hammond.
Me: Uh…Hi….Uh…as in …. THE John Hammond??
J.H.: Yes, you opened for me at the Iron Horse in Northampton a couple of years ago. Do you remember that?
Me: Uh, do *I* remember that? Yeah, of course. I'm surprised that you remember *me*. How can I help you????
J>H>: I'm doing a show at Castleton State College tonight and thought you might like to be my guest.
Me (breathless): Well, that's a very nice offer, but I actually have to host my best friend's birthday party (Mary McFall). Man, what a bummer!
J.H.: Well that's OK. Marla [delete (his wife)] and I will be staying in Rutland tonight and are planning to come to Manchester tomorrow. Would you like to get together for lunch?
Me (fainted…fell on the floor…woke up…got up off the floor…regained composure…): Yeah, sure, that'd be fine.
J.H.: OK, I'll call you when we're in Manchester.
Me (not really sure if this is for real): Wonderful, I'm very flattered at the offer, and how on earth did you ever remember me?
J.H.: That's Marla. She keeps track of everything for me. When we knew we were going to be in Vermont and near Manchester, which, as you know, is our most favorite town in the country and where we vacation every year, I said to her, "Didn't that guy that opened for us at the Iron Horse say he lived in Manchester?" and Marla found your card. It'll be great to see you.
Me (speechless): Uh…It'll be great to see you too, John. Thanks so much for the invite and for getting in touch. See you tomorrow. Click.

What a freakin' crazy world, eh? For those of you who do not know John Hammond, do a Google search. Or go to this link: http://www.rosebudus.com/hammond

[134]

I'll let you know what I have for lunch!

So as it turned out, I had a House Special sandwich. John, Marla, and I had a wonderful luncheon and conversation. After about 45 minutes or so, I thought it was all coming to an end when John said, "Marla's going shopping. You want to go to my car and listen to my new CD?" (His new CD "In Your Arms Again" was not coming out until Jan. 25, 2005. He had a demo copy. I was fortunate enough to be one of a handful of people to have the opportunity to hear it first.)

We hopped in his Nissan Maxima and drove around to various stores in town so Marla could go shopping while he and I sat and listened first to his CD, and then to my CD, "Made in Vermont." He gave my CD high marks. We talked about life, music, politics, and family. I asked him about his father and he told me a most remarkable tale.

It turns out that his father left his mother when John, Jr., was five. Raised by his mom, John, Jr., had little positive contact with his father. His father was born to a wealthy family and dedicated his life to assisting predominantly black musicians with their careers. He discovered Bessie Smith, Count Basie, Billie Holiday, Bob Dylan, Bruce Springsteen, Stevie Ray Vaughan, and others. He worked for Columbia records and would never take more than the minimum salary. He died poor.

I asked John if his father helped him with his start in the music business, and he said, "When I told my father what I wanted to do, he said, 'I don't think that's the right thing for you to do.' I didn't listen to him and I've been on the road for well over 40 years.

"One time my dad did call me was when I was 18. He said, 'John, I've got this girl from Wisconsin coming in to record today. You should come see her.' I went to the studio. [delete "I was 18" as you've already given his age.] The girl was black and beautiful. I had never heard anyone sing like her. It was Aretha Franklin."

[135]

My mouth dropped at the image. Two young kids—one singing, one listening—both of whom grew up to be entertainers. What a life this is.

Chapter 15

Sage Advice from Jerry Portnoy

Photo: Bob Stannard

There are few musicians who have had a greater impact on my work than Jerry Portnoy. It's not like I have been a real regular student of his or anything. I have had only four or five sessions

[137]

with the man. Still, whether he knows it or not, he has made a huge difference in how I play the harmonica, and, subsequently, how I look at life. The two go hand in hand.

Jerry Portnoy was Muddy Waters' last harmonica player. Jerry followed a lineup of harp players that included Little Walter Jacobs, James Cotton, Mojo Buford, and others. Chicago-born, this man is the real deal.

I was on vacation on Cape Cod and generally when I'm down there, I'll stop by Harry's Blues Bar in Hyannis. It's just around the corner from the Cape Cod Melody Tent so you never know who is going to pop in there. I have played with some incredible musicians at this venue, including Kid Bangham, guitarist for the Fabulous Thunderbirds, and David "Honey Boy" Edwards.

This particular night was Blues Jam night. I had my case of harps with me. I was standing around waiting for Ricky "King" Russell to start calling up players; generally not until the second set. I was leaning against a post at the "old Harry's" (they've since renovated the place) when suddenly standing next to me was a guy who looked real familiar but I couldn't place him. He was wearing a denim jacket with a big yellow sun over the left, breast pocket. Circled around the top of the sun, also in bright yellow stitching, were the words "SUN RECORDS."

This jacket did not come from Wal-Mart. As I'm standing there, wracking my brain trying to remember who this guy was, Ricky said, "Ladies and gentlemen, I don't usually bring players up on stage this early, but I have a special guest here tonight. Put your hands together for Mr. Jerry Portnoy."

OH MAN! Could I be a bigger dork? Here I was standing right next to one of the world's greatest harmonica players and I didn't even know it. Jerry did a couple of tunes and came back to where he had previously been standing. I introduced myself and engaged him in a conversation. I happened to mention that I had just released my first CD and I'd like to give him a copy.

[138]

"You have it with you?" he asked.

"Yeah, I have a copy right here in my harp case."

"Get it and come with me." I got the CD and was so taken aback at his abruptness that I left my harps right there on a table. In a million years I wouldn't leave my harps behind. I was possessed.

We left the club, turned left, and started walking down the street. Street lights were now behind us and it was pretty dark. We turned left again. "Jeez, is this guy going to mug me for a CD that I was already going to give him?" I thought to myself. Parked close to the curb was a pastel yellow 1993 Cadillac about a hundred feet long.

"Get in," he demanded.

I got in the passenger side. He got in the driver's side. "Let me see your CD." I gave it to him and he opened it. "Damn, I just got this car the other day. Guess it doesn't have a CD player. You care to hear my new album? It's not out yet. I just have it on a tape."

The album was "Down in the Mood Room." If you don't have it; go buy it. It's incredible. The tape starts playing. I'm thinking to myself, "Here I am sitting in Jerry Portnoy's new, used Caddy, listening to his soon-to-be but not yet released album. Someone kill me now. Life ain't getting' better than this".

There came a time in the first song when I heard a technique that I've heard for years but could never quite figure out how to do it.

"Hey, Jerry. How are you making that sound right back there?" Jerry backed up the tape and replayed the chop. "Yeah, that's it right there. How're you doing that?"

[139]

Jerry did what any self-respecting harp player would do. He fished around on his dashboard for the right harp (it's a boon not to be a drummer), put an A harmonica to his lips, and began to play along with his own song.

So now I'm sitting here with Jerry Portnoy in his new, used Caddy, listening to his soon to be, but not yet, released album WITH HIM PLAYING ALONG TO HIS OWN SONG. It's times like these when I am elated that I don't carry a handgun, because I would have been very tempted to kill myself right there. Of course, he would've been very angry at the mess made in the new, used Caddy.

In what may go down as THE most courageous moment of my entire life, I looked over at him when he stopped playing and said, "Ya know, there were times when guys like you would take guys like me and drag them along a little bit. You think you might be up for that?" I was fully expecting him to say, "Get out of the car." Instead, he looked at me. Stared at me. He was contemplative. I was terrified.

"I couldn't do it for free. It's partially how I make my living," he said after a very long pause. "OK, what do you need?"

We negotiated a deal and I said, "I'll be back down here at Thanksgiving. Can we get together then?"

"Let's talk when it gets closer," he replied.

I called Jerry the Tuesday before Thanksgiving and set up a session at 11:00 a.m. the Friday after Thanksgiving. "Oh, by the way, did you ever get a chance to listen to my CD?" I inquired.

"Yeah" was all he said. There was a very long pause and I asked, "What did you think?" There was another pause that took long enough for more wrinkles to form in my face.

[140]

"What would you like me to say?" Ouch. Another long pause and finally he said, "OK, I'll say this. You can benefit by spending an hour with me."

I think I would have preferred him to say, "You have a cancerous tumor and have three weeks to live." I knew right away that this was going to be a long hour. Masters of any trade tend to want to make you pay more than the going rate—not in money.

I drove to his house and parked in his driveway. Now, you need to understand that at this point in my life I had been playing harmonica for 35 years. I didn't think I sucked (well, technically speaking ALL harmonica players suck AND blow). I sat in my car and thought to myself, "I can't go in there. This guy is going to cut my head (an adage often uttered by old Blues guys when they are learning chops from other players. It means you're going to get your head cut). "Suck it up, asshole. This is the opportunity of a lifetime. Get your sorry butt in there."

I got out of the car and went to his porch door, which, of course, was locked. He was sitting on his porch smoking a cigarette; something I have oftentimes wondered about as a harp player, but many harp players do smoke. Hey, if it works for you. He invited me in. That was a good sign. We shot the bull for a minute and he said, "Let's go downstairs to my studio."

As if I wasn't anxious enough, walking into Jerry Portnoy's studio is enough to make any harp player drop to their knees. The walls are plastered with photographs of Jerry playing with Muddy, Clapton, Albert King, Albert Collins. You name it. There is a three foot high bookcase on the left at the bottom of the stairs. On top of the bookcase there are about twenty vintage microphones. "Nice mics. Where'd you get 'em?" I asked.

Jerry pointed to the microphones one at a time, "Little Walter. Big Walter Horton. Sonny Boy Williamson I. Sonny Boy II." On and on he went. These were the original microphones used by the best players of all time. I turned around and looked behind me. There

[141]

on the wall, framed and signed by everyone in the band, including Eric Clapton, was a gold record of "From the Cradle," the best Blues album of 1995. I had never seen a gold record before.

"Have a seat." His voice sounded like it was a thousand miles away. I snapped out of my memorabilia trance.

"What? Oh, yeah, sure." I sat on the couch. He sat in a stuffed chair to my left.

"Grab an A harp and play something."

Have you ever had anyone say to you, "Grab an A harp" and then immediately have your brain freeze? When someone who you've idolized for years says "play something" there is no way in hell you can think of anything to play. Brains don't work that way.

Now, try walking around a room with the most incredible display of Blues memorabilia you've ever seen and then have one of the best players of all time say "Play something." At that moment in time I had completely forgotten how to play. I did something, which must have sounded very similar to a donkey hee-hawing. I knew it sounded like crap.

"OK, stop. You don't know what you're doing."

Me without my airline barf bag. We went back to the beginning and he made me play the scales, as in Do Re Me. In 35 years I had never played the scales. I just played. I knew the notes were in there somewhere and I found them.

"OK, now play the scale doing tonguing.. It's helpful to note here that I am self-taught. I had never had a lesson with another player. Finding someone to give harmonica lessons in Vermont is tough. I proceeded with what I thought to be tonguing. It wasn't even close. It was this triple-tonguing staccato thing I do.

"What the hell is that?" he asked with a pretty stern look on his face.

I never wanted to run out of a room faster than I did at that moment. "Tonguing?"

"You don't know how to do tonguing, do you?"

Well, to be honest, I didn't know if I did or not. He showed me what he was talking about and as fate would have it, I could do tonguing, but not like Jerry.

My one-hour lesson flew by in about a minute and a half. We were cooking right along with Jerry showing me all kinds of things. I looked at my watch. An hour and five minutes had past. "Looks like my hour is up," I pointed out to him.

"My wife's out for the afternoon. What's your schedule?" I didn't have to be back to work at the Vermont State House until January.

"I got time." We kept going. Back and forth. He was showing me stuff I'd heard for years but just couldn't quite get down. This must be what it feels like to go to Mecca. I was in my glory.

The next time I looked at my watch, a little over four hours had passed since we began. I was stunned. Time is just such a bizarre thing. Drags on forever one minute, flies right by the next. "Geez, Jerry, I've been here all day. I owe you a fortune."

Jerry looked at me for what felt like a long time. We got by the opening hurdle of egos and fear (ego from him; fear from me) and were really having fun. I was anyway. I was prepared to write him a check for the full amount when he said, "Like I said, one hour."

With no mirror handy it was hard to tell if I turned white. Neither one of us spoke. I took a blank check out of my pocket, filled out the date. Made it payable to him for four hours of his time and handed it to him, folded in half. Jerry is a very smooth individual. He's very knowledgeable on a variety of subjects. He is a highly intelligent man and you can talk with him about anything. He spent his life around some of the greatest Blues players who ever lived. There is man who is not rich in terms of dollars, but has lived a remarkably rich life.

Before the check entered his pocket, I caught a glimpse of his thumb and index finger sliding the check apart just enough so that he could catch a look at the amount. He slid the check into his pocket. We never talked about money again. I go to see him when I can; not nearly often enough. He always charges me for a one-hour lesson. I think the briefest amount of time I've spent with him has been three hours. I write him a check for the full amount.

The following is an interview I did with Jerry for *Barrelhouse Blues Magazine*:

The author & Jerry Portnoy
Photo: self-timed. Bob Stannard

Jerry Portnoy Interview

Barrelhouse Blue Magazine

The best way to describe Blues harmonica legend, Jerry Portnoy is sophisticated and smooth. Jerry Portnoy grew up in Chicago and at an early age was exposed to the greatest Blues musicians the world has ever known. His father owned a carpet store on the famed Maxwell Street. But it wasn't until later in his life that success grabbed onto him and ran full speed ahead.

At the age of thirty he was tapped by Muddy Waters to be his man on the harp. The rest, as they say, is history. He formed the Legendary Blues Band and more recently is Eric Clapton's choice for harp players.

Aside from being one of the best technical players of all time (Muddy Waters declared him the best since Little Walter Jacobs), Jerry is arguably the greatest teacher of the instrument alive today. He has created the " Blues Harmonica Masterclass" instructional three CD series, in which he analyzes and breaks down the techniques of harmonica playing.

As is true with every Blues legend in America, Jerry Portnoy has led an amazing life…and it ain't over yet. You can learn more about him at his website: www.harpmaster.com

DTB = "Downtown" Bob

DTB: For a little background, you were born in Chicago. Could you tell us a little bit about what life was like growing up on Maxwell Street?

JP: My father had a rug and carpet business on Maxwell Street and he grew up there. I lived up on the north side of Chicago. I spent every Sunday on Maxwell St. That was the "big day" for the market and music.

DTB: Did you ever work for your father?

[145]

JP: No. Other than running errands for his employees, but it did allow me to hang around this area at a time when there were many great players there. I was only about five years old at the time, but the music seemed to resonate with me.

DTB: Where did the musical instincts come from?

JP: They were all pretty musical on my mom's side—cousins. A lot of artists. My mother played the piano and was a professional singer almost making it to the Lyric Opera. She made it through two auditions, but was cut at the third. She had a very good voice. Of course, on Maxwell Street there was always a lot of Blues to be heard. I firmly believe that those memories were captured at an early age; at a time when you're that young and your mind draws in everything like a sponge, only to have it come out later in life, twenty years later in my case.

DTB: How old were you when you first started playing.

JP: I was 24.

DTB: You tried a few other instruments before hitting on the harp. What else do you play?

JP: Yeah, I tried the piano, the guitar and the accordion.

DTB: The accordion is a tricky instrument to play, isn't it?

JP: Yeah, especially when you're barely big enough to hold the darn thing up. I was pretty much of a little shrimp when I was kid and they had,.... well, they had a lot more door-to-door delivery salesmen back then; ya know, the Fuller Brush men, encyclopedia salesmen and the like.

DTB: They had door-to-door accordion salesmen back then?

JP: Yeah! This was like in the early '50s. There was this guy, Dick Contino, who was like the Elvis of accordion players. He

[146]

was pretty famous. Was even on Ed Sullivan. He had dark, curly hair and was a real handsome guy. He could play the shit out of an accordion. He got into some trouble with the draft during the Korean War. He didn't want to go. It kinda ruined his career.

DTB: So you were exposed to America's finest music (the Blues) when you were five years old. Twenty years later did you stay in Chicago the whole time?

JP: (Laughs) Yeah.

DTB: Did the harmonica find you?
JP: I had been in the service and was out and I was running the largest pool hall in Chicago. In January of '67 I went to San Francisco. I was there for the "Summer of Love."

DTB: How'd that work out?

JP: Oh, that worked out pretty good. Then in November, I had an apartment up on the hill on 17th St. I was with this gorgeous blond. We had split up so I decided to go to Europe. I was 24. I was over at a friend's house, Brian Harrington. He was a guitar player. I noticed an A Blues harp on his mantelpiece. I took it down and started fooling around with you it, you know, and I had this epiphany. I had tried these other instruments, but they had never felt natural to me. I just had an innate sense that I could play it. It made sense to me. I was always doing something with my mouth. The low notes were on the left end; the high notes on the right end. All you had to do was to breathe in and out. It did not require any special dexterity with the hands and I thought, "I can sort this out." Brian said, "Take it with you when you go to Europe." I would play on the side of the road as I was hitchhiking...play Shenandoah or whatever came to my mind. The Blues was still buried in my memory, but nothing has triggered its release...yet.

I met an American guy in Spain who could play the Blues. I ended up in Sweden, crashing with this guy I knew and I went into a

[147]

record store where I found a Sonny Boy Williamson record. He cut it when he was in Europe in the '60s. I brought it back to the apartment, dropped some acid and listened to it. I never came back. [Laughs] I said that was the coolest shit I ever heard in my life. I gotta learn how to do that. From that moment on that was what I wanted to do. I knew I had to get back to the States where this music originated, but I didn't have any money.

As serendipity would have it, I got dragged in on this drug bust; I was part of a group that got pulled in for having some hashish. Make a long story short, I got a free ride back to the states. [Laughs] After some ups and downs.

DTB: That'll be another story for another time.

JP: It'll all be in the book. I got back to the States, went to California and met Sonny Terry.

DTB: Did you seek out Sonny Terry?

JP: Not really. I saw in the paper that he was playing at Mandrakes near Berkley. I hitchhiked over and got to the club early. I got a table right in the front. A while later I saw the stage door open and this lady leading in this blind man who I realized was Sonny. It was Emma, who Sonny later married. She asked me if she could sit at my table so she could be close to Sonny if he needed her. They both sat at my table and I started talking with him. I asked him if he ever gave private lessons and he invited me to stop by his hotel room. He was in town for a week. I went to see him with a tape recorder and did some work with him. We became quite close, in spite of the fact that I play nothing like him.

Shortly after working with him I decided that I was more interested in the Chicago style of playing. I went back to Chicago to be with my dad who was sick and later passed away.

DTB: Is it accurate to say that your first real lesson was with Sonny Terry?

[148]

JP: Yeah, as far as any real lessons I ever had. It wasn't like real teaching back then. These guys would just play what they know for you. It was up to you to figure out what they were doing. They'd just say, "It go like this," and then just play. But to be able to sit in the room with them and watch and listen to them and what they were doing, that made all the difference.

Sonny and I remained friends over the years and he was really glad that I did so well. I used to walk him over to Mandrakes. He had these shirts specially made for him that would hold his harps. One day he reached in and pulled out a harp and said, "Jerry, this harp has taken me all over the world. If you stick with it, it will do the same for you." He told me that I picked this stuff up quicker than anyone he had ever shown. He was a wonderful guy and fabulous showman.

DTB: I was going to ask who had the most influence on you. You mentioned Big Walter Horton.

JP: He was an interesting character. He had a crusty exterior, but was a real sweet guy inside. He used to live in this rooming house around 35th St. and I'd go down there wearing an overcoat and carrying a pint of VO in my pocket. I'd hold on to the neck and tilt it back to make it look like I was packing a gun and walked down the street with an exaggerated sense of "don't screw with me" [laughs] and hoped nobody would screw with me. It wasn't the greatest neighborhood.

I go over to his place, we'd crack the bottle and I would ask him about this and that and how did this go and he would just play. To this day, his sound—good lord, what a sound he had. He'd just show me how he'd played it. I had my cheap tape recorder....

DTB: You recorded him? Do you still have some of those tapes?

JP: Yeah...

DTB: Lord have mercy; that's very cool. You ever listen to them?

[149]

JP: Every now and then.

DTB: I got Sonny in a hotel room in Montreal and I got Big Walter in his rooming house in Chicago. He was playing solo. It was great.

DTB: Did you ever get to meet Little Walter Jacobs?

JP: No, I think he got killed in '67; just around the time I started playing

DTB: There's a big leap here from the time you met Sonny Terry and Big Walter to the time you met Muddy Waters.

JP: In 1970 after I got back from California I was going to clubs and I went to a club—the Quiet Knight up on Belmont St. At that time Paul Oscher was playing harp with him then. Paul is one of the most naturally talented musicians I've ever met. Just a talented guy with music running through him. A real natural feel for the deep blues. He really knocked my socks off. I met him during the break. He immediately yanked me into the bathroom and had me take out a harp and play something for him. He was surprised at what I could do. We became friends.

He was living in Muddy's basement at 4339 Southlake Park. Spann had lived there before him....

DTB: Otis Spann?

JP: Yeah. Anyway Paul was living in Muddy's basement and I'd stop by; pick him up and we'd go riding around. Sometimes we'd stop upstairs. Muddy would be wearing a silk bathrobe and his hair up in a do-rag and a bottle of champagne. He liked to watch the Cubs on TV. If he was in a good mood, he'd invite us to have some champagne with him. That's how I got to know Muddy before I ever got to play with him.

DTB: What if he was in a bad mood? No champagne?

JP: No champagne. But he knew I played and Paul eventually left the band in '72 and was replaced by Carey Bell for a while; then MoJo Buford came on. Meanwhile I was playing with Johnny Young; and then Johnny Littlejohn and Sam Lay...

DTB: Sam Lay the drummer?

JP: Yeah, he was the original drummer with [Paul] Butterfield and played with Howlin' Wolf. My playing was coming along.

DTB: So you're now playing out?

JP: I was playing in the Midwest with Johnny Young and Johnny Littlejohn. Illinois, Wisconsin, Michigan, Indiana, Iowa. I had a day job at this time. I was working at the Cook County Jail officially doing "Vocational Evaluation." To get this job you had to be a college graduate so I had someone forge a college transcript for me so that I could qualify to work in a jail [laughs]. It almost came home to roost in the end.

Johnny Young passed away in April of '74 and there was going to be a big benefit at this club called On Broadway. I put a couple of harps in my pocket before I went to work that day knowing I was going to go to the benefit after work. When I got there...I'll never forget this...it was a seminal moment in my life. I open the door to the club and the place was just packed. Way across the room I could see the bandstand and I saw Muddy at a table. I almost turned around and left, because the place was a madhouse. I looked up and I saw Muddy looking at me all the way across from the other side of the room. I could tell he was looking dead at me. He waved and motions me over. That was the equivalent of the Royal Summons. I elbowed my way through the crowd and Muddy says, "You wanna play my set with me?" I said sure, man. I had sat in with him a couple of times before. It always freaked me out; made me nervous. My mouth would dry out and I never felt I played my best. All that stuff.

[151]

DTB: Where was MoJo?

JP: He had quit the band, but I didn't realize that at the time. I thought that he just didn't make the benefit. At this time I had put my own band together and was playing at Buddy Guy's place on the South Side with AC Reed and Danny Draher. I was just starting to try to sing. For some reason I was particularly relaxed this evening as we did Long Distance Call and other Muddy stuff. I played real well. At least I didn't beat myself up about it.

In front of me Muddy says to his manager, "Get this boy's number." I knew how Muddy was. He was really cool and made you feel real good. He'd recognize you and make you stand up in a crowd to take a bow. Hey I was nothin' then. It made you feel real good.

I think he's just trying to make me feel good, but I'm on a high. I leave the club, standing under the awning because it's raining. I waited around to thank him for letting me play with him. He comes out and says to me, "Can you travel?" I replied, "Wherever in this world you want me to be; you just tell me and I'll be there." He said, You'll be hearing from me."

I didn't want to even go there in my mind. I didn't want to start trippin' on playing with Muddy Waters. I go home; I think it was on a Tuesday. I go to work the next couple of days and on Friday, I got home and the phone rings. It's Scott Cameron, Muddy's manager. As soon as those words came out of his mouth the mental computer started going. There was no freakin' reason in the world why this guy would be calling me except one. I can't stare it in the face; it's too awesome. He said Muddy wants you to call him. He said call Muddy and then call me right back. I called Muddy. He answers the phone (big, low voice), "Yeah?"

I said, Hey, Muddy, it's me, Jerry, the harp player.

"Yeah, well we start May 25th in Indianapolis; the boys will be playin' down at Queen Bees on the South side this weekend. You should go down there to get familiar with what we're playin'. That's it."

I'm standing there holding the phone and I don't know what to say. Holy shit! I think I said something like, "Thanks Muddy" or "I'll talk with you later." Or something. I have no idea. I still couldn't let loose. I had to call his manager, which I did and told him what Muddy had said.

He asked me if I had a passport, to which I replied I did not. He said, "Get one. We're going to France next month, the Riviera."

I said, "This is solid, right? No chance of this falling through, right?" I told him I had to quit my job. He said Muddy's word is as good as gold.

It was only then, after I hung up that phone, that I could let it all out. I started screaming. I threw the door open to my apartment and ran off (leaving the door open) and just started running down the street. The energy was rising up in my chest. I ran up Broadway. I had to tell somebody. A friend of mine owned this little record store about three blocks up. I just burst in and said, "Ed, I just got hired by Muddy Waters." I was beside myself.

DTB: How old were you?

JP: Thirty.

DTB: How long were you with him?

JP: Six years steady.

DTB: Did you leave or did he leave?

JP: No, the band left him.

DTB: Bad circumstance?

JP: That's a really long and involved story. Let's just say that we had some managerial issues and leave it at that.

DTB: What happened after you left?

JP: We had some really good success with the Legendary Blues Band.

DTB: Somewhere along the line you must have met [Eric] Clapton.

JP: Yeah, we were his opening act in Europe in 1978.

DTB: You must have been freaking to open for Eric Clapton?

JP: The Clapton thing didn't bother me. Clapton was just some English rock star. I didn't give a shit about that. I'm standing next to Muddy Waters! What the screw!

At the end of Clapton's shows he would call Muddy and me out to play with him. That's how I got to know Eric the first time around.

DTB: The second time around?

JP: Well, uh, some time went by. I had the Legendary Blues Band....

DTB: Who was in the Legendary Blues Band?

JP: Pinetop Perkins, Willy Smith, Calvin Jones and various guitarists; Louis Meyers who played with Little Walter; Duke Robillard; Billy Flynn.

DTB: You still in contact with these guys?

JP: I just did a show with them recently in Spain. I still talk with Paul Oscher.

DTB: So the circle is still there.

JP: Oh yeah, but we're getting old. Pinetop is 94 and he's still at it. All we can do is keep going.

DTB: Before we wrap this up I'd like to know your views on where you see the Blues headed. Is it over? Still have legs? Where's it going?

JP: It's time in the forefront is certainly past and I don't think there's a way to bring it back. That said, however, it remains a constant underpinning of American music. The social factors that made it Black America's popular music no longer exist. But like I say, it is still the underpinnings of America's music. That will always be so.

Chapter 16

Learning to Negotiate the Vermont Way

Rufus Lake lived in a shanty next to his mother's shanty. We never knew her name. No need to. She already had a name. It was Gramma Lake. If she had teeth it was not clearly evident to us kids. Rufus Lake was a fixture in my town from the time I was old enough to know people, which would have been in the mid-1950s. Rufus had a barn (sort of) next to his very small shack of a house. The floor in his house was not dirt like houses where I lived growing up. He had a real floor, but it was tiny. The buildings in which he and Gramma lived have since disappeared, right along with the rest of life. When I drive by the site where their houses once stood I am still amazed that two people lived in such small quarters. You make do in Vermont and if you can settle for less, you'll do alright. Rufus and Gramma Lake knew how to settle for less. They seemed to do alright. They were both always very happy to see the kids.

I heard Steve Wynn's soon-to-be-ex-wife say that there are two kinds of freedom. There is rich freedom and there is poor freedom. Steve Wynn of Las Vegas mega-hotel(s) fame likes rich freedom. Most likely that's why he's about to have an ex-wife. Rufus and Gramma Lake much preferred poor freedom. It's a lot less complicated.

Rufus wore an old, floppy felt hat that was brownish grey in color. It was probably white when it was new. Not many of Rufus's possessions were new. As a matter of fact, I would guess nothing he owned was new. He wore work pants and a work shirt, which always showed signs of sweat. His boots were worn, but seemed to suffice. If they didn't, we sure wouldn't know, because I don't think anyone ever heard him complain about anything. Of course, he never did say all that much. He would sometime get a little animated at his horses and beat the crap out of them if they acted up. It made quite an impression on the kids. When we were with Rufus we never acted up. We weren't nearly as tough as those horses, and they didn't look like they had a lot of fun going on when Rufus beat on them.
I was too young to know much about Rufus's past life or if he ever did anything, like for a living. All I ever knew that he cut the

hay in the meadows around South Dorset, which pretty much no longer exist as they have been replaced by houses. Rufus would cut the hay with a non-motorized sickle bar. This machine would sit dormant until it was hooked up behind the ever-obedient horses. When the horses walked forward the wheels of the machine would turn and the gears would cause the sickle bar to slide back and forth. No carbon footprint was left behind by this process, that's for sure. Once cut and laid dry for a day or two, all the kids in the neighborhood would help him load the hay on his flatbed hay wagon. The wagon had side walls on it, but they weren't tight. That is, you could see through them. They were more like a railing. We would hand rake the hay into piles and fork the piles up on the wagon. The older kids got to use the forks for fear of the younger kids spearing themselves in the foot, which would have been inevitable. I'm not sure if Rufus ever got paid to do this or if he just got to keep the hay for his two giant draft horses. Kind of a revolving cycle deal. Got two horses that need to be fed. Go get some hay and feed the horses. I always figured he could have saved a ton of work by just getting rid of the horses, but what did I know. I was a kid.

After spending most of the day raking and forking hay, we would get a full load on the wagon. We would then all hop aboard and Rufus would head north toward Dorset—the opposite direction from where he lived. We would plod along Rt. 30 right smack in the middle of the road. Rufus never had any intentions of pulling over for anyone, not that there was all that much traffic on Rt. 30 in 1958. We would go up to the center of Dorset, around the Dorset green, and then back down south on Rt. 30, clogging up the traffic going the other way.

It may not sound like much but this was about THE most incredible adventure a kid in South Dorset in the '50s could imagine. As an aside, our parents never had much of a clue about what we were doing. There was no paranoia about "OH MY GOD, WHERE ARE THE KIDS?" The kids were with an old man who drank a ton of beer while we helped him collect hay. Years later I figured out that he rode around in that hay wagon because it was much safer than driving and he was right. He didn't have a pot to piss in or a window to throw it out of, but we all looked up to him, if not with adoration, then perhaps with amazement and a little fear tossed in.

Negotiating with someone can change the way you feel about them. When I was ten my dad bought me a brand-new Barlow knife. If you are unfamiliar with Barlow knives, it's because you were raised in the city. You are more familiar with the colorful switchblades, which are, of course, completely useless for anything other than killing people. In our wildest dreams, we could never envision a scenario where we would want to kill someone here in Vermont. Animals, maybe; people, probably not. Back then it seems we got along better.

Anyway, I've got this new Barlow knife. It was the first new knife I had ever had. You had to have this knife if you were going to be a Boy Scout, which was the plan. I was carving and whittling up a storm. Cutting things. Carving things. Messing around with the screw driver and the can opener. Man, what a great knife. Not long after I got this knife I saw Rufus out in a field. I had to go show him my new knife. He was a man of few words. Never did say all that much, but we always seemed to know what he wanted us to do.

"Hey, Rufus, take a look at my new knife," I said as I hauled out my new Barlow. I opened up the large, main blade; the smaller blade; the can opener. They all glistened in the bright sunlight.

"That's quite a knife you got there. Brand-new is it?" he said.

"Oh yeah, I just got it the other day." "It's a good one," I said. "I don't know if it's as good as the one I carry," he said, and proceeded to pull out his pocketknife. I had seen this knife once before, a long time ago. It had real bone on either side (not plastic like the Barlow). It was a real beauty. Any kid would kill for that knife, if, of course, we'd ever kill here in Vermont and as a rule we wouldn't.

[159]

I stood there in the hot sun staring at Rufus's knife. It was hypnotic. The tiny, shiny steel rivets that secured the genuine bone to the frame reflected the sun right into my eye. I was done for.

"You want to trade?" he asked. Wow. All I had to do was say YES and I had a one-of-a-kind-riveted-bone-handle knife that belonged to Rufus Lake. I was about to be the proud owner of his knife. I was on the threshold of being the envy of every kid in town. My friends would be amazed that I negotiated the sweetest deal ever and got this knife away from Rufus Lake.

"YES," I said, and held out my knife with all the blades still open.

He carefully took my knife, snapped the blades closed, and slid it into his pocket. He placed his knife in the palm of my left. I will never forget the feeling I had at that precise moment in time when I looked down at my then little, wrinkle-free hand and saw that magnificent bone-handle knife. At that moment I was the absolute coolest person on the planet. I could not believe that old man would have been crazy enough to trade that wonderful knife with genuine bone for my plastic Barlow, even if it was brand-new. I just knew I got the better end of this deal.

A good deal is when both parties believe that they have screwed the other party to the wall like a piece of plywood. Both parties think they've won. Once the knife was in my hand I decided I better hightail it out of there before the old guy sobered up and changed his mind.
"OK, Rufus. Thanks for the knife. See you later," I said nervously and turned to leave.

"Pleasure doing business with ya," he replied.

I had the knife in my pocket and I was holding it; fondling it all the way home. I waited until I was home, safe and sound, before I took it out of my pocket and began to explore it. I tried to open the blades only to discover that all of them had been broken off. There

[160]

was nothing but a broken stub left of each blade. I never did have the heart to go back to him and call him a cheat and a crook. I thought it over and came to the conclusion that this was more my fault than his. All I had to do was look at the blades right there before we made the deal. Nope, instead I was sucked into a deal by the glitz and glitter, and, of course, the fabulous feeling that I had screwed him to the wall like a piece of plywood. I realized then that he was probably feeling the same way.

Rufus and I never once spoke about the knife for as long as he lived, but it was always between the two of us, and things changed from that day on. Whenever we had a load of hay and went for our ride up to Dorset and back, he always let me sit next to him on the bench seat of the wagon. The bench seat was usually reserved for the bigger kids. The little kids always rode in the back on the hay, pretty much because that was a lot of fun. The first ride after the knife deal, he just looked at me and I looked at him. I was thinking, "That old bastard screwed me out of my new knife." Reading my mind, he smiled just a little bit (he was never big on smiling much) and tipped his head towards the empty space on the bench seat right next to him.

As you can see, learning how to negotiate at an early age is a good thing. Vermonters have a way about negotiating. First, they size you up. Then they take you for everything you got. Then you get pissed 'cause you got screwed blind. Then you realize what a good guy the guy was who screwed you. Then you buy him a beer. He buys you a beer. Life is good. Perhaps we should send some Vermonters over to Israel and Palestine or maybe Afghanistan to do some negotiating.

Looking back I think I did end up getting the better of him. I would have just cut off my fingers with that Barlow anyway. Then how would I have ever been able to type or hold a harmonica. See how things always turn out for the best if you let them?

[161]

Rufus Lake
with kids that
he loved,
nearly as much
as his horses.

Chapter 17

Running for Office in Vermont

(What Else Would You Do in Recessionary Times?)

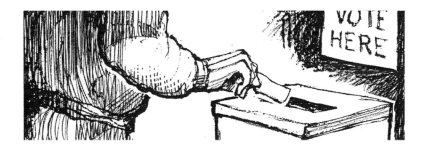

In tough economic times, when there is no good work to be had, the next best thing for you to do would be to run for office. OK, it's a bit stressful and requires you to be 100% fully certifiable but the paycheck will clear.

In 1982 I decided I was going to run for public office. The year before, I was tapped by the Select Board of Manchester, Vermont, to fill out the remaining terms on the Planning Commission and the Bennington County Regional Planning Commission. I found this somewhat amusing since, generally speaking, I had never had a plan. Experience has shown that plans rarely go according to plans. Through the appointment process, presumably consisting of the board tossing a coin, I found myself serving the public.

You don't fully comprehend just how many public there are until you begin serving them. Let's just say, for the record, there are many of them, they all have an opinion, and they all feel compelled to share their opinion with you. This is fine. It goes with the turf. What they don't tell you is that the turf is everywhere you go, any time, any place. Those of you considering going into public life take heed and remember this: try very hard not to get caught on camera in your running suit with your hair perfectly intact like that dufus Rob Blogojeyich did. Or your mom will be very angry.

I was about to mow the lawn in Dorset where the New York City girl sat a year or so before when I saw the lawn's owner, Joe Allen, lying in his multi-colored, plastic, webbed outdoor lounge chair, sunning himself. He did that a lot. He had a great tan. He also had the most perfect teeth I had ever seen. That is generally a dead giveaway, by the way. Folks showing up here with perfect teeth need not wear the sandwich board declaring that they are from out-of-state. We know.

Joe Allen owns a few restaurants around the world. He was one of the few "transplants" who understood Vermont. He wore army fatigues and drove a Volkswagen. (After he'd been here a while, he drove a Morris Minor. It was the same make car I drove in high school; his was in better shape, however.) If his teeth hadn't been so straight and white, we would have never known he was from New York City. Plus, he never really said much, which is also always a good thing if you're trying to blend in. Actually, it's best not to ever say anything, but that is sometimes impossible, like if your car goes off the road and you have to tell the Vermonter who is about to yank your car out of the ditch just exactly where to hook the chain on your SUV. FYI—the bumper is never the right choice.

I unloaded my mower and before starting it up, I walked over to Joe, who was lying down reading a book. I was standing there looking down on him. He was looking up at me. I guess he thought I was going to say, "Hey, would you mind moving the chair out into the street so I can mow your lawn," but instead, I said, "I'm running for office."

I've spent almost thirty years wondering what must have rifled through his head when I said that. Did he think to himself, "Senate?" "Governor?" "President?" "Please, God, let the police show up right now and take this man off my property?" Fortunately, there were very few cops around then.

There are many reasonable responses to the statement I posed to Joe, such as, "WHY?" or "Are you nuts? You would never win." Instead, Joe said, "Are you going to keep a journal?"

Say what? I asked, "Why?"

"People down where I live might find it interesting to learn about what it's like to run for office in Vermont". No kidding!? I was thirty years old and never thought that anyone anywhere ever gave a crap about what happened in Vermont, because, for the most part with few exceptions, no one living here really gave a crap about what happened here, because as the new T-shirt so aptly states, "What Happens in Vermont Stays in Vermont. But Nothing Ever Happens in Vermont."

"I hadn't thought about it, to be honest with you. Guess I could."
Joe moved his chair off to one side as I mowed the spot where he
had just been. That was it. Like I said, Joe was a man of few
words. I'd bet money, if I had any, that he had some Vermont
blood in him.

Thanks to that terse exchange I ended up keeping a journal, or a
log, or whatever. I jotted down some notes of what I was doing. I
went back and read them over and decided that there was nothing
you'd care to hear about. I mean, who would want to know about
a young guy driving around seven Vermont towns in a 1960 Willys
Jeep, with a custom metal cab that was covered with giant faded
decals of a bear, a deer, and a trout, and with an exterior shiny
chrome stack exhaust pipe that came right up in front of the
driver's door and exhausted the fumes over the top of the cab?

This one-of-a-kind piece of transportation formerly belonged to
Leonard "Slim" Pelky. Slim worked at the local car wash. "Slim"
was a cheerful and gracious man. Always a smile when you saw
him. His smile was extra big for me, I suspect, because he thought
he screwed me to the wall. Little did he know about my expert
negotiating skills with Rufus. I got to know Slim pretty well. He
was really a good guy; a local character who was always quick
with a smile in between taking a drag off his cigarette and sipping
his coffee.

The district that I hoped to represent was a two-member district.
Each State Representative in Vermont represents approximately
3,000 to 3,500 people, which usually makes up about three towns
or, in your case, one apartment building. Since I was in a two-
member district, using quick math skills developed at an early age,
I had twice that many. It would have been hard to know all of
them by both their first and last names had I not been related to
most of them.

Those of you who are Vermonters can pretty much skip over the
next few pages, because I'm going to tell what it was like to
campaign for office in Vermont, riding around in an old Jeep with

[166]

faded decals and a pretty hip side-stack exhaust pipe. You already know what it's like to ride around on dirt roads and talk to your neighbors, so feel free to move on.

For the most part, the feedback that I got when I'd pull into someone's driveway was pretty positive. I'd hop out of the Jeep and hand out my brochure and announce that I was a candidate for office. "No way? You look smarter than that," they'd say. Or, "I thought that job was reserved for the village idiot. Oh, right, you ARE the village idiot."

Running for office anywhere is not easy and I admire anyone who gives it a go. In larger states it's easier. You have a campaign staff that schedules you to appear at certain functions. You are kept far, far away from the crowds, so as not to have embarrassing moments or to be forced to exchange bacteria via handshaking. You make a speech and are whisked off to the next event. Under extreme circumstances, you may have to kiss a baby for a photo opportunity. A staffer is generally fired immediately afterwards.

What a luxury that must be. In Vermont it's just the opposite. The candidate is right out there naked in the wind, and believe me, when you're running for office in Vermont, there is a lot of wind. It comes from the people who have been harboring pent-up emotions about all the things that have been wrong with Vermont since the Revolutionary War. Now if you think I'm pulling your leg here, go file yourself a petition.

I first got exposed to the process of campaigning thanks to Rep. Bob Graf (R-Pawlet). You may remember him from the poker game a while back. I was attending my first Bennington County Republican Committee Rubber Chicken Dinner. It was really chicken. I'm reasonably sure it was not real rubber. Bob sat right across the high school cafeteria table from Alison and me. Those were the long tables that mysteriously folded right up and disappeared into the wall like the Murphy bed in your apartment.

Alison is from the Boston area and, shall we say, slightly more upscale than me. She, too, had been born to parents who were Republicans. I think I can say with certainty that she didn't find the idea of my running for office as a Republican nearly as amusing as I did. Less than a decade before, we were hippies. This was a tough adjustment for both of us. Fortunately, I have a stronger sense of heritage (and humor).

It's hard to tell what tipped the scales for Alison regarding her dislike for appearing in public at events, like the one in which we found ourselves that evening. I mean, she's fine with just hanging around with most folks, even Republicans.

I'm going out on a limb here but it might have been that during the entire meal, right from the salad straight on through the entire chicken core-don-rubber-blue, Bob Graf never once took his chew of tobacco out of his mouth. I know what you're thinking here. No point is wasting a good chew. Years later I came to realize that keeping that wad of chew in the entire dinner help to disguise the taste of the chicken. Like I said earlier in this book, Bob had been in the House for twenty-two years. He didn't survive that long by being anybody's fool. He must've been to hundreds of these dinners and finally figured out how to get through 'em.

Having learned the basic fundamentals of how to get through a Republican County dinner I was on my way to becoming a candidate.

Chapter 18

Door to Door

Many strange and interesting things happen when you run for office. The only way to get elected to the General Assembly in Vermont is to campaign door to door—going to every door in your district. The hardest thing in the world is to go to the first door of the first constituent. Candidates have been known to freeze solid as they raise their hand to bang on that first door. Should it be a rarely used door, it could be months before the body would be discovered.

The subsequent few thousand are a breeze, but that first one is a killer. It took me several days to muster up the nerve to approach the home of a total stranger and tell them why I should be the one to represent their best interests in the State House and what great things I would do to not only change their life for the better but to change the world. I was very optimistic. Years later I did change parties, which had no impact on their lives nor did it make the world a better place. It did rile up a few, though.

I was in my extremely classy '60s Willys Jeep—the one with the decals and smokin' smokestack. I pulled into this stately mansion (my district was comprised of the richest of the rich and poorest of the poor.). It was way back off the road. So far, in fact, that I had driven past it my entire life and had no idea it was there. I drove into the long, winding driveway to find a huge brick house. The front door was open (it was pretty warm even though it was early in the morning). The inside door was open but the screen door was closed. I could look through the house and see the sprawling backyard.

I shut off the Jeep and got out. I had taken about two steps when all hell broke loose. A black Labrador retriever that was probably ten years old and had been overfed from the day it arrived at this lovely home came running right at the screen door. Of course he's going to stop. Nope. He jumped barely high enough to clear the metal piece on the bottom and blew that screen door to pieces. This was one happy dog. He appeared to be taken aback at the idea of being free. Right behind him was a little white thing that posed as a dog. It would never survive rabbit season if let loose.

The little white thing posing as a dog struggled for all it was worth to climb up over the metal bottom of the blown-out screen door. He was a persistent little bugger and made it up and over. Within seconds there were two dogs running around the driveway like crazed banshees.

I was hoping that they would regain their senses and get back in the house. No such luck. The blown-out screen door flew open and there stood the lady of the house. She wore a maroon and gold paisley housecoat that brushed the ground. Her hair was up in some sort of matching, funky turban. We are not used to seeing outfits like this in Vermont. In her right hand was a cigarette in a long, black cigarette holder. She looked like a Greta Garbo knock off.

"Come here dogs! Come here dogs!" she bellowed in what I interpreted to be a heavy German accent. It was pretty apparent that she did not have family in the ground. The dogs had a much different plan. They were running left and right like a pair of big black and small white pinballs. The dogs were flying around. The lady was screaming. I thought to myself, "This is going well."

Then, with a snap of her head, her attention was directed straight at me. "Who are you and vat do you vant?"

I walked right up, big as you please, putting on my best Vermont candidate face. "My name is Bob Stannard and I am running for State Representative," I declared as I handed her my flyer with my left and stuck out my right hand for her to shake.

I quickly learned that hand shaking was not customary in her country. My right hand hung out there for quite a while when this mysterious, albeit grumpy, lady said, "I do not vote. I am not a resident uf dees town. I am not even a resident uf dees country."

Spotting an opening, I simultaneously retracted my outstretched right hand as I snatched the flyer out of her hand (running a

[171]

campaign in Vermont can cost upwards of a hundred bucks or so, so you can't be wasting those flyers) and said, "Thanks for your time! Best of luck with the dogs." I turned and made a beeline for the Jeep, which, thankfully, started up with the first turn of the key. I believe that the Jeep wanted to leave this place as badly as I did.

I got out alive. The dogs are still running, no doubt.

Chapter 19

Going Where No Man Has Gone Before

I had a meeting with Rep. Bob Graf (R-Pawlet) to talk about part of the legislative district I hoped to represent. This two-member district included the southern Vermont towns of Manchester, Dorset, Danby, Peru, Mt. Tabor, Landgrove, and Winhall. (Note: Winhall is also known as Bondville. Don't ask. It's a Vermont thing.) About sixteen years ago the district was split up. Manchester is now a stand-alone district, with the other towns divided up elsewhere. Danby and Mt. Tabor went back over to Pawlet, from whence they had originally come. They are still looking for Winhall/Bondville.

At any rate, Graf was telling me all about Danby and Mt. Tabor and how they were "different." "What do you mean by different?" I asked.

"No point in telling you unless you win," he said. "In the meantime, you're going to have to campaign in both towns, and I might suggest that you go see Hugh Bromley, a local farmer. You can't win Danby without Hugh." He gave me directions. They sounded ominous. Go up the mountain a ways. Turn off the mountain road onto a dirt road, which will take you to a side road (not to be confused with a "dirt road," although it, too, is dirt), which should take you to his driveway (provided you made the right turn at the tree). His driveway goes on for a bit. It's also dirt.

I considered bringing provisions. I was driving a 1963 Plymouth Belvedere wagon. It was a real cream puff; well, except for a tiny bit of rust behind one wheel well. For you unfortunates out there who have never had the privilege of owning a '63 Belvedere, suffice it to say that there is no way you could drive this car today in Vermont without wearing a flack jacket and the side panels reinforced.

People in Vermont would run you out of town for driving a car that gets only 14 mpg. The one obvious noted exception here is if you're driving a spanking-new, all-wheel drive, freakin' HUMMER. For reasons most native Vermonters have never figured out, many of Those-from-Away seem to find the

[174]

HUMMER their car of choice. Why would you have a rig too freakin' wide for any log road in Vermont? They're stuck before they leave the highway. Many Vermonters think that they are owned just for show. We seem to think that the smaller the driver, the larger the car. It's somewhat sad to watch the little dwarfs struggle to see out the windshield. They'd be much better off with a '59 Willys.

I was intently following the directions given to me. They might as well have been in French, because I was hopelessly lost before I left the house. Me and my pristine Belvedere found ourselves on what I hoped was the driveway to the Bromley farm. The road was dirt and not all that wide. The Belvedere, however, WAS quite wide…and low to the ground. It was never meant to be off pavement and here I am practically 4-wheelin'.

CRUNCH was the sound of my perfectly lovely and unblemished (with the exception of a bit of rust) Belvedere bottoming out; a term used to describe what occurs when a moron takes an appropriate car on an inappropriate road (see section on Dad's driving). CRUNCH again. And CRUNCH again. After about the third bottoming out I was commencing to take on what you might describe as an attitude. I was swearing like a parrot about this godforsaken piece-of-crap road when I froze at what I was seeing coming down the road.

A milk truck with a stainless steel tank is one huge truck. It goes around the state picking up milk from farmers who live in the most godforsaken places on earth. When was the last time you saw a farm conveniently located in downtown? These milk truck drivers risk their lives every single day just so you don't have to drink black coffee. The drivers, whose collective nerves are shot by the time they are in their early thirties, hope you are happy.
There was no way that this milk truck and my stunning Belvedere (with miniscule rust) wagon were going to get past each other on this one-and-a-half-lane road. I was at least a half mile up this blasted road and I was not about to back down (backing down when 4-wheeling demonstrates a disconcerting sign of weakness.

[175]

We would prefer simply to kill ourselves than ever use the "R" designated on our stick shift. (Note: For obvious reasons, since we can't say this word, we can't type it either. This is most likely where J.K. Rowling got the idea for "He-who-cannot-be-named".) I had no idea how far it was back to the farm, but it didn't matter. The milk truck was going to have to back up.

This particular driver of this particular truck was an older gent. He was way past the stage when his nervous system had been destroyed by driving the backroads of Vermont. To quote Pink Floyd, he was "Comfortably Numb." He had no intention of backing up. Coincidentally, he had no intention of slowing down either. Or pulling over, for that matter. It all made perfect sense. His vehicle was as big as a house. I either moved or died. It really wasn't much of a decision for him. Vermonters have the ability to look at things myopically.

I pulled WAAAAAYYYYYYYY over to the right. I could see my life pass before my eyes. This was not going to work. Mr. Threadtheneedlewithmygianttruck didn't seem to be nearly as concerned. He kept coming right along.

Dying while on the campaign trail was not what I had bargained for, but I was taking solace in the fact that I would have received a positive and supportive headline in the press. FIRST-TIME CANDIDATE FLATTENED BY MILK TRUCK. DRIVER SAYS, "NEVER SAW HIM."

Our respective fenders came within inches of each other. "I think we might have this," I thought. CRUNCH. I was really getting sick of this sound. I watched as my driver's side exterior mirror exploded. I could see my distorted face with a horrifying expression reflecting on the stainless steel tank in which the milk was sloshing back and forth. I was praying that it was sloshing back right about now as forth would only aggravate the situation. Neither of us stopped. We weren't going fast, but we both refused to stop. Once in motion, stay in motion. I was grateful that I had only lost a mirror. I continued on my way. I looked down at my

[176]

fingers only to realize that blood had not circulated through them for some time now. I was fixated on the remarkably pale color of my skin when I was snapped out of my trance by another CRUNCH. That was five now. My fingers were regaining their color. I was coming around.

I crested the hill and was treated to one of the most beautiful, panoramic views in a state full of beautiful, panoramic views. It was a 300 degree view looking northwest, north, east and southeast. It was breathtaking.

This proved to be fortunate, i.e., not having enough breath left in my lungs, because had there been any air left, it would have been displaced by reflex action due to the scene that now displaced the panoramic view. There stood three men: one older, two younger, and with what appeared to be rifles. My fears were unfounded as I learned that they were only shotguns. I was pretty nervous, but, hey, I was a candidate. Neither rain, nor sleet, nor snow, nor milk trucks…uh, right, different job. Pays more. Better benefits.

I got out of the once-lovely Belvedere, brochure in hand, and approached the three seemingly hostile-looking men. I say "seemingly" because I had no doubt that deep inside, these were kind and caring men. I was hoping to discover this side of them prior to having my brains blown out.

"Hi, I'm Bob Stannard, and I am a candidate for State Representative," I ever so boldly declared.

"We don't want no politicians on our land" was the response. I knew immediately that I was a long ways away from the kind and caring side of these thoughtful, if not somewhat territorial, men.

"See that lovely, beautiful, pristine, gorgeous (notwithstanding some minor rust) 1963 Plymouth Belvedere? I have practically smashed it to smithereens getting up this freaking road and I'll be dipped in dog crap if I'm going to just turn around and leave without talking to somebody about something."

[177]

"Looks like we got a live one here, boys." These were not overly reassuring words and sounded hauntingly familiar. I think they were spoken in the movie "Deliverance." Hey, wait a minute now, these were MY PEOPLE. I should be able to communicate with them.

"So what's on your mind? Did you say your name was Stannard?"

Name recognition goes a long way here in Vermont. If you are thinking of moving up this way and your name is, oh, say, Sodenberg or Costanzia or Czycskzysck, you might want to consider changing it to Stannard. Life might be easier, however, if it ever comes up, to just say, "No, not THAT Stannard" and you'll be fine.

Now that we broke the ice, we got to talking about deer hunting and what not, and it turned out that he had a real issue with people trespassing on his property. I said that I thought there were already laws on the books covering trespassing since we've been trespassing on each other's land since the Indians arrived, but that I'd look into it if elected. We were getting along. I had a chance to meet the lady of the house, who one could easily tell by her accent was not from here. She was a very nice lady who had come to Vermont to live with her husband after the War (WWII). She did not, however, give up her citizenship (one less vote). After about an hour and a half of chatting and gawking at the view, I decided it was time to go.

"Well, young Jim Stannard (if Vermonters cannot remember your first name, even if it's on a brochure, but they knew your father or grandfather or his father, they will refer to you based on the last one of the family that they knew), let me tell you something. I haven't voted in over thirty years, but I just might go vote this year."

What? After five bottom-outs and a destroyed mirror and fourteen heart attacks, I find out this guy doesn't vote? "Graf," I thought to myself, "you're a dead man." I got in the once-pristine Belvedere and drove straight to see Bob Graf. I told him of meeting the Bromley family. I said, "Graf, you son-of-a-bitch, you sent me all the way up to hell and gone to see a guy with a wife who is not a citizen and the guy doesn't even vote. What the hell was that about? I oughta kill you right here."

"Oh, no, they never vote," he said, "but they do talk to everyone."

As it turned out, Mr. Bromley did vote that year. I carried Danby every time I ran for office, even after I changed parties. I fixed the mirror, thanks to the help of a local junk yard. It all worked out. It usually does.

Chapter 20

Man of the People

Once elected, it was now time to serve. Serving actually makes campaigning look somewhat like Sunday school. As previously mentioned, I represented seven Vermont towns: Dorset, Manchester, Danby, Mt. Tabor, Peru, Landgrove, and Winhall (Bondville). At the time, Landgrove was the wealthiest town per capita of any town in the state. Not sure just where Danby and Mt. Tabor fit in, but I can assure you it was light years away from Landgrove. From one end to the other, this district covered 67 miles. It was about the size of Switzerland. If you were to stop a Vermonter who was busy pulling someone out of a ditch in Danby and ask, "How do you get to Landgrove?" he would reply, "You can't get there from here." That's one of the quaint Vermont colloquialisms that you've heard about, which in this case is factual.

In 1982 I described Danby as a town that stopped in time around 1950. It was a rural farming town consisting of hard-working, hard-playing people. They could be a rough bunch but some of the finest people you ever met. Very funny people, too. If you don't think so, try representing them in the legislature.

I prided myself in attending the Town Meetings of all seven towns I represented. For you city folks who might not be familiar with Town Meeting, it's pretty simple. It's democracy at the lowest common denominator—as it should be. Annually, on the first Tuesday of March (more or less), people come out from their winter hibernation to reunite with their friends, whom they've not seen since Thanksgiving, to decide the issues before the town. Sometimes the niceties quickly wear off and these meetings can be somewhat cantankerous. As a rule, the more cantankerous they become, the happier we are that we showed up. You have to attend one to appreciate the sheer delight of watching your neighbors fight to the death over whether or not the town should fix a pothole.

At any rate, the first Town Meetings I attended outside of my own town proved amusing. I attended four on Monday night and the remaining three on Tuesday. (Some towns meet the night before the first Tuesday. Others meet on Saturday.) On Monday evening I would go to Dorset, Manchester, Mt. Tabor, and Danby, in that order.

I would generally wear a suit and tie. At the very least, I thought it a good idea to look like a legislator, even if I had my doubts about whether or not I really was one. I raced from town to town. The Danby Town Hall is conveniently located on the top of Danby Mountain Road at Danby Four Corners. It would be hard for you to find Danby Four Corners, even if you were standing right at the crossroads, as it's actually only three corners. One of Vermont's greatest mysteries (aside from the disappearances in Glastenbury) is the naming of a "T" intersection "Four Corners."

I nervously walked into the Town Hall, which was packed with local Danby folks. Although you enter the front door, you come upon the backs of the people in the room. There were a couple of guys I knew hanging out toward the back of the room, near the front door, who looked at me in my suit and tie. "What are doing wearing a tie here?" one guy asked. Before I could answer he continued, "You'll be lucky to get out of here alive wearing that outfit." (Note: After learning the dress code for this meeting, in subsequent years I would bring a change of clothes with me. After attending Dorset's and Manchester's meetings, I would drive the 13 miles to Danby while peeling off my suit and tie and changing into jeans and a flannel shirt. If you have not figured it out by now, serving the public in Vermont has its challenges.)

These words offered in friendship did little to alleviate my anxieties. The moderator was a cheerful chap named Gil Raynor. He had flowing white hair and a pencil-thin moustache positioned decisively under his nose. He looked a little like Clark Gable. He had a great speaking voice, which is handy if you want to be Town Moderator. Gil was a Flatlander, proving once again how open and accepting Vermonters can be. Presumably, he either carried a concealed weapon or paid his bills on time, or both.

[182]

"I see we have our State Representative here with us tonight, and as you know, in order for someone not from Danby to speak to this group, it requires a vote of the body. Would you like to hear from your representative, Bob Stannard?" was the question he put to the group.

It is more than slightly unnerving to have an entire town of people gathered for their annual ritual of Town Meeting to collectively and in unison shout at the top of their lungs, "NOOOOOOOOOOOOOOooooooooooo!"

Without so much as a twitch he continued, "Hearing no objection, I will now turn the meeting over to our State Representative Bob Stannard." I had been campaigning all over this town for months and knew just about everyone in the room, at least by their first name. I was related to half of them. What the hell just happened here? I had no idea if he was serious or kidding. My first appearance before this town, in which I had won handily, had just unanimously been voted down! I took over the podium and addressed the crowd. "I-i-i-it's always a pleasure to here with my friends in Danby," I said, still shaking.

It takes a keen, well-trained eye to notice when a Vermonter is being funny. The difference between being funny and not being funny is negligible. If you hold very still and stare (but without staring, rather like looking at a dog; don't look into their eyes), you might notice one side of the mouth twitch upward ever so slightly. I thought I observed this phenomenon on at least three of the 70 or so people in the room. I quickly realized that I could be on safe ground.

Over the next six years, I would receive the same reception each and every time I appeared before the town. When asked if they would like a report from Montpelier, they would all vote (loudly) not to let me speak. There would be a short pause and Mr. Raynor would turn the meeting over to me. As a lifelong Vermonter, even I found this local custom somewhat unique. I have heard my own town say "No" to allowing its State Senator a chance to speak, but they weren't kidding. He wasn't allowed to speak. I don't know of any other town that said "No" with such passion and then allowed the emotionally crippled politician to go ahead. This offers yet another good reason why you should be reading this book. You probably thought that they'd say "NO" just the first time.

When I had been a State Representative for three years and was making my third appearance before this town, the opening reception was the same as it had been the previous two years. However, this year things would be different. This year, the legislature was considering a bill that would allow the state to step in and take over planning and zoning for a town that did not have a Planning and Zoning Department. Danby never saw much need for such things as they all tended to their own business. Saw it as a waste of time, I guess. It's not, really, but that's how they saw it. Bringing change to a Vermont community not really wild about change can sometimes result in an uprising. Uprisings are rarely a good thing. The Civil War comes to mind. There have been some uncivil wars as well. Best to avoid them, too, if at all possible.

I came to the meeting prepared with a stack of 3 x 5 index cards with specific notes on the various components of the bill that was before the legislature. After receiving my customary warm welcome I said, "Hey now folks. You're going to have to pay close attention here, 'cause this year we have a pretty darn serious piece of legislation that's going to have a real impact on this town." No one seemed particularly alarmed at my alarm.
I proceeded to go through the points neatly handwritten on my cards. I was about 60 seconds into my presentation when I looked out over the sea of relatively disinterested faces. The scene reminded me of the movie "One Flew Over the Cuckoo's Nest." I took a deep breath and said, "Perhaps this might be a good time to see if anyone has any questions." I was good at reading a room.

There was a large man in the back of the room (or front, depending on whether or not you came in the front door) who took a few tries to get up from his hard, metal chair. He wore a black and red wool shirt and a large wallet chained to his belt. One would think he was pretty wealthy 'cause he seemed worried about losing that wallet. He finally got to his feet and raised his hand high in the air.

"Yes, you sir, in the back. You have a question?"

[new graph]"Yeah, I do. What do you do to make your head shine like that?" he asked.

I'm balder now than I was then, but I was pretty bald then. I stared hopelessly at my little 3 x 5 cards desperately trying to find the answer to his question. I looked up into the crowd. No one appeared to be laughing, although they most certainly were. I looked at their collective mouths trying to see if there was a twitch to be had anywhere. It was a great moment for them. It took me a while, years actually, to determine that it was a great moment for me, too. Best to be able to laugh at yourself, because if you don't, others will laugh much harder.

It was one of the few times I was caught flat-footed in public. I just stood there. I'm sure I had an expression similar to that of Lee Harvey Oswald right after he was linked for all eternity with Jack Ruby.   After probably only a few seconds, which felt like a few years, a lady off to my left, with her hair up in rollers covered by one of those trendy, plastic bonnets with little flowers on it, held her hand high in the air.

"Yyyyes, you ma'am. You have a question?" I asked more than a little anxious. When I was very young, my older brother, Jimmy, dared me to pee on an electric fence. Guarded but confident, I peed on the fence. The feeling that I was experiencing at this moment was somewhat like that.

"Yes. I want to know if you're going to run again. You voted for mandatory seat belts and I'm thinking of running against you."
Yup, this was about like peeing on that fence for a second time.

"I have no idea. I don't make that decision for months from now. But I'll tell you what; you'll get more votes in Danby than I'll ever get." That drew a chuckle from one or two folks. "Does anyone have any questions about the subject at hand?" I begged, hoping that someone, anyone, was paying attention to what I was saying.

It was at this moment that the Chair of the Selectboard turned around, looked at me, and said in a voice loud enough to be heard over in Mt. Tabor, "We ain't gonna worry too much about those boys from State. You just send 'em down here and we'll blow their freakin' heads right off."

"Well, alrighty then. It's always good to be here with my friends in Danby, and if you should ever have any questions or trouble, please don't hesitate to call me." People from Danby, for the most part, prefer to keep their questions to themselves. If they ever do have any trouble, they pretty much know how to resolve it themselves, too. Your best bet is to just let 'em alone. That formula has worked well for about 200 years or so. We've been known to say here, "If it ain't broke, don't fix it."

To this day Danby doesn't have zoning and I don't think the State has ever come into Danby to "help" with planning and zoning. Things seem to be going along fine in Danby today.

Chapter 21

No Apologies Necessary

Whether you work at Wal-Mart or you're a legislator, it's important to keep in good with your boss during hard times. This lesson was learned the hard way many years ago. Valuable lessons learned will help you get through the recession, which, of course, is why I'm writing this book.

OK, rule number one. Don't ever, EVER, tell your boss that he/she has made a mistake. If you see that they have made an error, take the blame yourself. Hey, you're just a worker/legislator so you're probably a screwup anyway. That's why you're not the boss.

The upside of being a legislator is that you are elected and therefore can't be fired for two years. Two years is about as long as anyone in Vermont stays at one job anyway, so this could be viewed as tenure. Not having to confront the fear of being fired allows you the freedom to do the dumbest things imaginable. Here's proof.

In February of 1983 the legislature was going through its ritual of confirming judges. This is an amusing procedure in which a joint session of the House and Senate is held for the sole purpose of rubber-stamping the governor's recommendation for judges. In many states judges are elected, which means that it's a political process. Not so in Vermont.

All were assembled in the House Chambers for this prestigious event. A list of judges for confirmation was on each desk and handed to Senators who get to sit in the regal, red chairs and gaze out over the members of the House they believe to be inferior. The feeling is mutual.

The task at hand was to simply check the box of the judge(s) up for confirmation. How hard is that? If you are me, it's somewhere in between climbing Mt. Everest and swimming to Cuba.

I recognized the name of one of the men on the list who was to become a judge. I did not know the man personally. I only knew that at one point he represented a town that was considering buying a landfill for what seemed like cheap money and that he had counseled the town not to do so. I didn't know if he was a good guy or bad guy or if this was a good call or a bad call. Some of the folks I talked to thought it was a bad call, but that's all I knew. Not a lot to go on, but more than enough to practically hang myself.

I scrolled down through the list and his was the only name I recognized. "Gee," I thought to myself, "nobody asked me about this man." So, I wrote a note to then Gov. Richard Snelling that read, "Dear Gov. I think you might be making a mistake in recommending this man as a judge." This was my attempt at being helpful. I didn't want the governor to make a mistake. Of course, the name was already on the ballot and there was nothing that could be done about it at this point, but never let inevitability get in the way of sharing unwanted advice.

I called a page over and asked that he deliver this note to the governor right away. About 10 minutes later the poor freckle-faced boy came back to my desk looking like he had put a bobby pin in an outlet. "The ggggggovernor would like to see you in his ooooffice," he said, his voice cracking.

"Jeez, why so nervous?" I thought. I got up from my seat—seat #8, right in the front row—and walked out of the proceedings in front of the entire room, full of dignitaries, and headed toward the ceremonial office the governor uses when he/she is in the building. What happened was not all that ceremonial.

I was escorted into the large office with very high ceilings. Ancient paintings adorn the walls. Behind the ceremonial desk hangs the largest mirror in the building (presumably so that whoever is governor can get a pretty good look at him or herself). Looking straight into the office, along the far wall is a long conference table that has been there through many governors.

Seated at this long table on the left was Governor Snelling. His suit coat was off and draped over a chair. His sleeves were rolled up, exposing his muscular arms—the arms of a one-time boxer. He had really big hands as well. His half-glasses were resting precariously on the end of his nose. Oddly enough, he did not look happy.

At the far right end of the table sat his lawyer. His lawyer did not look well. I suspected that he might have the flu as he was sweating profusely, in spite of the fact that he was completely motionless and the room air conditioned.

Between the two men, wadded up into a nice neat little ball, was my note. "Have a seat," Governor Snelling said, sounding more like a command than an invite. "Got your note," he said, his head tilting toward the wadded up piece of paper in front of me. I was beginning to comprehend why the unusual amount of perspiration dripping down the attorney's face. "Why don't you tell me why I'm making a mistake in this appointment," he said, looking very stern. This was not good. It might have been easier if I hadn't known Governor Snelling was once a boxer.

"Well, I don't know if I have anything specifi—" and before I could finish that sentence he said, "I would like specifics."

"Uh, er, um, well, as I understand it, he suggested to the town that they ought not to buy a landfill that seemed like a pretty fair price to pa—" and before that sentence was completed his attention whipped to the end of the table, where the perspiring lawyer sat, looking more like a person being filmed for a hostage video.

"Had you been the counsel for the town, what would you have done?" the Governor asked.
"I would have most likely offered the same advice, Governor." I started to get a very clear understanding of how the last few minutes of my life were about to unfold. I never wanted to leave a room more than this one right now, but I wasn't going to go anywhere. I was frozen solid.

[190]

"Do you have another example?" the governor asked.

"No, but what I would say is that going forward, it would be nice if, before recommending someone for a position like this, you contacted someone from the district." When people get angry they have the ability to turn a very attractive shade of red.

"I did consult with someone from the district," he said, his teeth clenched tightly together. Years later I would be reminded of those clenched teeth when my wife was in a bad car accident and broke her jaw, which had to be wired shut. It was like that, only tighter.

"And might that have been Madeline Harwood?" (Yes, Mrs. Harwood was the wife of Doc Harwood—the man pretty handy with a scalpel.)

"As a matter of fact it WAS Senator Harwood," he said, his eyes glaring at mine. Our noses were about 14 inches apart.

"Do you know the relationship between Senator Harwood and this judge?" I asked, thinking these could perhaps be the last words I would ever speak. I could feel little rivers of water running down both sides of my body. I had this perverse feeling that I was really bonding with the lawyer at the end of the table.

He yanked his glasses off his nose and threw them on the table near the crumpled note. "No, I do not. Perhaps you would like to enlighten me as to their relationship" he snarled as he inched closer to me. A left hook could not be far away and that would, thankfully, be the end of this living hell.

"My understanding is that he represented Senator Harwood in the recount of her last, close election in which she won by something like 70 votes. Maybe if she had lost, she might not have recommended him." OK, I know that was weak, but it's hard for a dying man to come up with much of anything in the final moments

[191]

of life. I was proud of myself that I was able to A) speak, and B) do so without a diaper.

Once again, time stood unnervingly still, but it could not have been more than a few seconds. I glanced to my right just to see how the lawyer was holding up. It appeared as though he died so as not to have to serve as a witness to the murder that was about to take place. I braced myself for a killing blow to the head that I had no ability or desire to attempt to block. It didn't come.

Instead, Governor Snelling sat back in his chair, moving away from my face and giving me hope that I might live.

"You're new here, right?" he asked. Wow, could he tell just by looking at me?

"Yeeee, yesssss, yes sir," I stammered.

"I have apparently taken an action that caused you, as a freshman legislator, to write this note of concern. Young man, I owe you an apology."

"Uh, no, Governor, gosh, uh, no, that's OK, uh…really…uh….there's no need…uh."

"OK, you can go now," he said abruptly. Just like that it was over. For me, at least. His attorney wasn't going anywhere. I got up, knees shaking. There was no offer to shake hands or anything like that and that was OK with me. I left the office and entered the well of the House.

A few members had to have noticed me when I walked into the House, looking a lot like that freckle-faced Page; the one who looked like he'd put his finger in an outlet.

To this day I have a Pavlovian feeling when I enter the governor's ceremonial office. I see the late Governor Snelling and his lawyer sitting there and fear sets in like a horse that's been spooked by a snake.

Watch Out for Snakes

At the age of six I started living with horses. Mom and Dad bought our first horse, Princess. Princess needed company (and Dad needed a horse to ride) so along came Blaze—a feisty chestnut with a shocking, white streak down his face. Other horses followed but none with more personality than these two. They were friends from the day they met and god forbid if you tried to take Princess out for a ride without Blaze. He'd cry and cry and once even jumped the fence so as not to be without her.

We kept the horses in a pasture right next to our house. I remember the grass in the pasture nibbled down to about the length of the greens at Mt. Anthony Country Club, with one exception. There was an area in the southwest section of the meadow just to the left of the barn. It couldn't have been more than twenty-five feet square. Here the grass grew up two feet tall. There was a distinct line where suddenly the grass was chewed down.

One day I asked my dad about this grass. He told me that a day or two after we got Blaze, he was spooked by a snake in that spot. He never went there again and oddly enough neither did Princess or any other horse we ever had. None of them. Once one horse decided that one small place on this earth was taboo, that was it for the whole bunch of 'em.

I remembered this as my wife, Alison, and I were coming back from a Blues show in Great Barrington, Massachusetts, yesterday. Great Barrington reminded me a lot of Saratoga. It's a beautiful town, as are Lenox and Stockbridge. We got talking about how nice these places are compared to some other towns in the area. We talked about how some areas of the same town may vary a lot (the "other-side-of-the-tracks" syndrome) and wondered why that is the case.

[193]

Is it like being born into wealth or poverty? People born into
wealth seem to stay wealthy for generations (the Kennedys,
Forbeses, Rothschilds come to mind). Likewise, those born into
poverty tend to stay where they are. Some who work incredibly
hard may find that they can acquire wealth, but I don't believe it's
the norm and I know that it is not easy. It takes enormous drive
and conviction. On the wealthy side, slackers may find that they
fall from wealth, but the family money usually pulls them out.
Going neither up nor down is easy to do.

To change one's situation, it is helpful to understand how and why
you got there. Early on there had to be one thing that caught the
attention of one person (or maybe a group) and that one thing was
enough to have him or her say, "This is where I want to be."
Contrarily, it may be that "this is the place I DON'T want to be."
It could've been the mountains, a lake, or some environmental
feature that caused our ancestors to make a decision. One thing is
for sure, it wasn't always this way. I mean, at one point the planet
was covered with dinosaurs, right? Who knows, maybe there were
areas that they refused to roam (were spooked) too.

We began to wonder what happened so many years ago that turned
the Lenox of yesteryear into the Lenox of today; and Manchester
into Manchester and Pownal into Pownal, and why one section of
Dorset is so much different from another section. We speculated
as to the turn of events that brought the Lincolns to Manchester
and the who-knows-who to Great Barrington and marveled at the
serendipity of it all. And whether or not it is true that once it's
done, it's done. Once one place has risen up, will it always stay
that way or can it fall back? Or can a town that has always been in
poverty pull itself out or is it destined to remain poor through some
cruel twist of fate?

We concluded that it's a lot harder for a poor community to rise
than for a rich, successful community to fall, only because getting
the attention of those of means to invest in a very poor community
is, well, really hard. The poor, generally speaking (and that's what

[194]

I do in this column—generally speak), want to be rich. The rich, unless I'm mistaken, don't generally want to be poor.

We also decided that this paradigm is really silly. Think about how rich all of our lives would be if we could all live more closely together and share each other's ideas and experiences. It's as silly as leaving that tasty green grass alone, because you were scared by a snake many years ago.

September 3, 2007

Chapter 22

You Scratch My Back

Rich is in the eyes of the beholder. You need to have money to be rich. Remember McCartney and Lennon telling you that "Money Can't Buy Me Love?" In the event that you are either too young or too old to remember the Beatles, let's make this easy for you.

If you had a ton of money and you invested it all with Bernie Madoff, you would be feeling bad right about now. Obviously, this did not happen to you because you were able to buy this book. What happened to those folks was truly a shame. Screwing people as Mr. Madoff did is not good. Madoff is lucky that my old friend, from whom I purchased my land, did not invest with him.

You might like to know how some do business in Vermont. Years ago people came to Vermont to rape and pillage the place. We passed laws to protect the land and drove them away. Others have tried to exploit the place only to discover that it's easier to fight a war in Afghanistan blindfolded. Then there are those who tend to play nice. More often than not, they are the "locals," although let's not be naïve. There are some locals who'll take complete and thorough advantage of their neighbors. Fortunately, we know who they are and shy away from them like a horse spooked by a snake. Some not familiar are at the mercy of trial and error. Others have survived. You might, too. One-hundred years from now it won't matter much.

Near the end of my mowing career I got a call from a man named James Montague. He was an artist and looked the part. He had thinning hair, occasionally combed straight back when it wasn't exercising its right to fly around at will.

Under his rather long nose resided a pencil-thin moustache like the one Clark Gable wore. The locals just knew him as that eccentric artist guy, but he was pretty well known and was a fine painter. Toward the end of his life he got into these crazy, outdoor sculptures that are difficult to describe. They were very colorful. Metal (or plastic) rods going this way and that with colorful stuff hanging off them. I thought they were cool. His longtime friends,

[197]

who considered him to be this la-de-da painter, were frightened. It made me like him all the more.

Jimmy, as he was known to his friends, called me one spring and asked if I could give him a price to take care of his lawn. He had a rather hideous lawn that sloped downhill everywhere, unless you were at the bottom, in which case it sloped uphill. It seemed to go on forever. I don't recall what I came up with for a price but apparently it wasn't enough to discourage him from hiring me and I must've thought it was fair. That's all that matters.

I began by doing his spring cleanup, which consisted of replacing about two-thirds of the dirt road on which he lived, back up on the road from whence it came. We cut the lawn each and every week until the leaves came down. Jimmy's place was surrounded by giant hardwood trees that dropped enough leaves in the fall to cover Detroit. We raked them up and added them to the compost pile that I had been creating for years.

Before you doze off here I should mention that I never sent him a bill for my services. As we were cleaning up his place that fall, he came out wearing this wonderful old, original, brown fedora and waist-length jacket. His moustache was perfect.

"Bob, I have never received an invoice from you. I must owe you a lot of money," he said with a slight tremble in his voice.

"Oh yeah. A fortune," I replied and went back to raking. Not knowing quite what to do, he stood there for some time while I pulled on the rake, combing the stubborn wet leaves from his lawn. I let him stand there for a bit and finally I said, "You're an artist, right?"

"Yes, of course. That is what I do," he said.
"Well, I'm an artist, too," I replied. "Every week I turn your lawn into a thing of beauty, do I not?"

"Oh, yes, yes, my place looks beautiful always" he proclaimed.

[198]

"OK, well how about we just swap my work for your work?" I don't think he was a starving artist, but I do think that all artists think that they are starving artists. Given the opportunity to part with cash or their artwork, they will generally choose their artwork.

"That would be wonderful," he said.

"Great, let's talk later in the fall." I always preferred that my customers remain in the house, because it would take longer to shoot the bull with them then it would to cut their grass. My desire to gab would oftentimes anger the crew, which was unfortunate because Alison was part of the crew. This could make for uncomfortable dinner conversation.

As they always do, the leaves did their thing, turning into crazy colors and then drifting on down to the ground, only to be raked up and carted off. Not unlike how life goes. When we were done with raking up all of his leaves, which took a crew of about 10 half a day, he came out and inspected the job. "My place looks very nice. I would like you and Alison to come to my house in two weeks on Sunday," he said firmly, more like a command than a suggestion.

The day was grey. Heavy dark clouds hung in the air. The days were getting shorter and colder. It was late afternoon as we stepped onto his porch, held up by white columns. We entered through a hallway that had "old" written all over it. Wood, wallpaper, and dark was what I recall. The house was built around the time folks first started coming up here. They must've heard that the Indians who inhabited the place knew how to party and thought they better get up here right away. More disappointed flatlanders. In spite of their disappointment they did build nice places. We were escorted to a room to the left where two stuffed wing chairs awaited.

[199]

Alison and I had never before been invited to the home of an artist for the purpose of viewing his work. It was a pretty upscale affair for us. I wore a Harris Tweed jacket and tie. Alison, who looks fabulous in anything, also was dressed up.

We sat in our respective seats. We sat up straight. In front of us was an empty easel. "Would you like some tea?" Jimmy asked, with his head tipped slightly to the right and his fine, smooth hands holding on to each other.

"Tea would be great," I said.

As tea was served Jimmy said, "Now, I am only going to show you a few pieces. Looking at too much artwork in one sitting is not healthy. One can get confused and frustrated. I am going to show you pieces that were done at various stages of my life. Don't focus so much on the individual piece as you should on the different style and techniques," he explained.

This art business was more complicated than I had contemplated. This was going to take some time. Spending time with Jimmy was a great way to spend time. If you stop right here and go back to the beginning of this book, you will recall that we all have about 25,550 days to invest. We were investing well this day.

We fell in love with each and every painting that he brought out and displayed on the easel. He showed us only six paintings, each one better than the next. Did we want to go with his early work, which he did when living in the south of France? Did we want one of the remarkable collections of paintings that he did on commission for the 1939 World's Fair in New York? He did a painting of a seaplane landing right there at Wall Street. Another of people of the day walking past caged animals in the zoo. Not only were they beautiful paintings, they were American history.

We were exhausted and, yes, confused and frustrated and we had only seen a handful of paintings. "How many do you have?" I asked.

[200]

"Come with me," and we went into his basement where he had all of his work separated by the periods of his life. If time had stopped forever while I stood in this one spot, I would have been the happiest man of all time. Time, however, does not play along with humans.

Jimmy quickly flipped through painting after painting after painting. There must have been hundreds of paintings. We darted through the World's Fair series, the still lifes, the landscapes. It was dizzying. "I would like you both to come back next Sunday. I would prefer that you not decide today."

Whew, that was close. I would prefer not to decide today, too, since there was no way that I COULD decide today or probably EVER. We said our good-byes and went back to our place, about two miles away. All that night Alison and I went back and forth between this painting and that one; this series and that one; this style and that one. It never once dawned on us what the price of any given painting would be.

We went back the following Sunday after having concluded that we wanted to re-review some of his earlier still-life work. He was thrilled that we had narrowed our search and brought up a few pieces for our inspection. We decided on a piece that he'd done when he was quite young. Vegetables on a tablecloth with a paring knife. I told him how much he owed me. Based on what he sells his work for, he decided I had two paintings coming.

We repeated the same process the following year. We raked, cut, and raked some more, and when the days grew short and the skies turned grey, we went back to Jimmy's house. We got all dolled up, had tea, and looked at more artwork. This time we decided on a dark painting of a café in the south of France. It's an incredible piece of work that blooms into life when a beam of light lands on it. I do regret not having chosen one of his World's Fair pieces, but I was never dissatisfied with the deal.

[201]

After receiving the second painting we were all even. I was nearing the time when I was going to be selling my business so this relationship was about to end. The story should end right here. Like most good stories, it doesn't.

Just before Christmas, after we had picked out our second painting and hung it where it remains to this day, we heard a knock on the door. Our dog went off like a bark-alarm. I went to the door to see the brown fedora with a nose protruding from under the brim. I opened the door. The head supporting the hat tipped back. There was the moustache in all its glory, meticulously trimmed, with Jimmy right behind it.

He had something in his hand. It was square and wrapped in brown paper. "Come in, come in. Don't stand out there in the cold." It was the first time he had ever been to our home. I have no idea how he found the place. It was long before GPS machines. He stood inside our kitchen and looked around at all the stuff (junk) that we have hanging from the beams that hold up our second floor.

"Have a seat," I offered.

"This is for you," he said as he handed the wrapped square to Alison. She opened the gift, which was an etching of a rose. The actual etching is about 4" x 5". It's plain but very detailed. In the lower right hand corner it reads, "Montague '33".
"Hey, Jim, you didn't have to do this. This is over and above our deal."

He replied, "You were both so enthusiastic about my work and it was such a pleasure to be able to show you what I've done and to have you sit there so politely," he rambled on. "I want you to have this."

Of course, the piece is wonderful, but it is the handwritten inscription on the back that brings us both such joy. "This etching was printed at the studio of Monsieur Galanis of Monmartre, Paris, on a press given him by Monsieur Edgar Degas; a press used by Degas before his blindness. To Alison and Robert in appreciation of their appreciation. Jimmy Montague – 1982."

This was the year that I sold my business. We would see Jimmy around town occasionally, but the "special relationship" that we had with him ended on that brilliant, cold December day.

Chapter 23

Forests and Trees

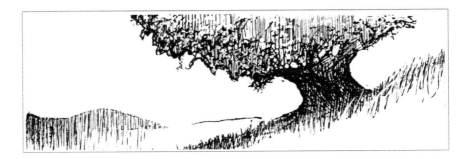

While you're sitting there on the verge of suicide after having lost everything you own, let me take this opportunity to tell you to just stop right there. Yes, it's bad out there, but how bad is it? What's the absolute worst that can happen?

You lose everything you own and end up living in a van down by the river with a guy who looks too much like Chris Farley? Alright, that would be pretty bad, but just remember; it could always be worse. Once you accept that simple fact, then you are on your way to surviving the financial meltdown that you find yourself in today.

That wasn't so hard. Oh, you say your van doesn't run? That fat guy sleeping next to you isn't nearly as beautiful as the babe you once slept with back when you had a small fortune? Odds are she didn't love you anyway. She loved your money. You'll be much happier in the long run. Try to get the guy sharing the van with you to bathe once in while.

Not only are you depressed at having lost everything in the recession, but now you're looking down your nose at others less fortunate than you.

"I was born to good stock. This can't happen to me," you say?

Vermonters (and other poor folks) wake up every morning knowing that they are a hairsbreadth away from being the guy you look down your nose upon. Many have been there right along. The difference is while your eyes were crossing as you stared down your nose, we were busy accepting folks for who they are. (Kindly refer back to Chapter 9.) We tend to be a forgiving and tolerant people, but we've been known to make exceptions when necessary.

"Forgive my ass!" you can be heard screaming as they drag you from the rooftop of the penthouse apartment you once owned, until you gave all your money to a guy named "Madoff," who made off with all your money. You're not in a very forgiving mood right now and we can understand your overreaction at having lost everything. It sucks. So what? You want to take it out on others? That's an option, but not a good one. All that'll do is compound the problems that you think you have into real ones.

Let's look at the situation a little more closely. You made a ton of money. That was your first mistake. Turned out a ton of money wasn't enough and you needed two tons, which you were able to acquire by working 22 hours a day, seven days a week.

Lo and behold, two tons weren't enough and you decided you needed ten tons. This "Madoff" guy was showing a good ROI (in Vermont we recently learned that ROI stands for "return on investment." We always figured it was for some idiot who couldn't spell ROY). Zombie-like, you turned over your fortune to a crook who, in turn, lost all your money and now you are mad at that guy? Perhaps you should go find a mirror and get mad at the guy you see there instead.

Either way, looking down on people who are down is not an uplifting thing to do. It tends to make others feel pretty bad and doesn't do much for you either. Oh, sure, you get to think for a brief period of time that you're better than this guy or that guy, and as long as you can stay on top, I suppose that's just fine.

But we're in a recession and the "top" has become more like a pointed needle with a very few left standing up there. It's now time to adjust. It's time to start looking up instead of looking down. You did something right to become successful, but you made a few hair-brain mistakes. You think you're the first person to make a mistake? Just make sure you aren't the LAST person to make a mistake. You want to try real hard not to be that guy; not that there's anything wrong with being last. Who knows, that person may the happiest of us all.

Now that you've lost everything, you will find that you have more freedom than you could ever dream of. The crushing burden of wealth has been taken off your shoulders and you have the freedom and mobility to get ready and knuckle down to being poor. You almost screwed up and invested all your bucks with someone who wasn't Bernie Madoff, someone who would have made you even more money. Then think of the trouble you would have. You would have made ten million and that wouldn't have been enough; you would've had to have twenty million.

You came dangerously close to making a lot of money and losing a life. Now that you're broke you can consider yourself one of the lucky ones. Again, to quote the soon-to-be-ex-Mrs. Steve Wynn, "There is the freedom of being rich, and the freedom of being poor. Steve prefers the freedom of being rich." Until he pays off the soon-to-be-ex-Mrs. Wynn, after which he is sure to have given up a little bit of that rich freedom. Perhaps after a few more ex-wives and Bernie Madoffs, he too will join the ranks of those rejoicing in the world of poor freedom.

Sometimes it's hard to see the forest through the trees.

To quote that old rocker, Huey Lewis, "It won't really matter much 100 years from now."

Trees

I do a fair amount of driving and I spend some time on I-89. I've made this trip hundreds of times over the past three decades, but last week I noticed something that I had to have seen on every trip but never registered. Trees.

Before you think that I've finally fallen into the abyss of late-middle age, let me assure you that I think I'm fine (that's probably the last thing one says prior to stepping off the ledge). There are sections on the side of this interstate that consist of nothing but rock. This is true of just about every road in Vermont, but I'm talking about what I saw here on this road.

Interstate-89 was built in the 1960s; not all that long ago for some of us; a lifetime ago for others. Trees have grown up over the nearly five decades since the ground was ravaged, ledge was blasted and pavement laid down to make our journey through Vermont all that much more enjoyable and faster.

I'm not talking about the beautiful trees in the median strip or the lovely forests that soften the view left and right. I'm talking about the skinny, scrawny, desperate trees that have sprouted out of the solid rock and are clinging on for dear life. It's one of life's marvels to think how a seed can travel through the air, land in the crevice dividing stone and somehow spring to life. It goes without saying that these poor, unfortunate trees are not nearly as robust and healthy as the other trees that had the good fortune of landing in the rich soil that lies elsewhere.

It appears to matter little to the dwarfed trees that their entire life's work consists of simply hanging on for dear life as others pass them by at speed unimaginable 100 years ago. Are they angry that their fate was determined by a howling wind? Are they disappointed that they would never be like the other, bigger, more handsome trees?

The trees that I finally had noticed vanished within seconds. They remained in my rear-view mirror only a moment longer. They caused me to think about people I have known from all walks of life; people who have lived a life of good fortune and people who have lived a good life with very little.

There are many who have achieved success (whatever that means) due to their social status. They had to do little more than be born into the right family. There are others, many more, who might have been successful had they not been born into a world of poverty. Some of the fortunate ones who live in a stratum of life where the "little people" seem of little consequence may look down upon these less fortunate people. They have it all. Resources. Good upbringing. Opportunities galore. They have hope for a better future. They may have all of this simply because they were lucky at birth.

The poor have little. They don't get to live life; they get to cling to it. They have no resources. Their upbringing may have been weak at best. Opportunities are few. Hope wanes with each passing day. But cling they must if they are to survive another day. In our country it is possible for one of few financial resources to achieve great things. It is by no means easy. To elevate from abject poverty to a financial success takes remarkable drive and determination. You have to be smart, determined and fight every step of the way. You cannot be discouraged even for one minute; say nothing about one day. You can't feel sorry for yourself because of the bad cards you were dealt. You have to achieve the impossible as you watch others speed right on by.

If you put up the best fight possible, the odds of success are probably still against you. For the more fortunate, at times it seems that they have to do nothing more than to get dressed in the morning and the day will just fall into place, for the seed responsible for their existence had the benefit of landing in good earth with nutritious soils.

It all seems so random, doesn't it? I have known fortunate people who seem to take life for granted. It doesn't make them good or bad, but it affords them an outlook that others cannot have. I have known many more less fortunate folks for whom life is a struggle. On average they tend to be slightly more cheerful. It's hard for them to hold on yet they get by. They want what they need and need what they've got. They have managed to cling to the rocks and against all odds somehow survive.

It may be easier and more pleasant to gaze upon the majestic, healthy trees and ignore those other poor, destitute trees growing out of rocks, but it shouldn't be about being easy. Sometimes we really don't see the forest, because of the trees.

March 28, 2009

Chapter 24

Start to Get Ready to Commence to Begin to Plan

Fortunately for you, we are nearing the end of what was intended to be a book on living through a recession that devolved into a bunch of useless stories of my life. I don't recall there being a guarantee with this book.

"If you want a guarantee, buy a toaster," I believe is how the old line goes. The guarantees of today are substantially different from those of a generation ago. Back then, you'd just bring whatever it was you bought back to where you bought it, and the guy who sold it to you was most likely the guy who was going to fix it. Think of what our kids have missed.

Today, you buy something, it breaks, and you send it to a little place 437 miles northeast of Beijing. The turn-around time is a little longer, I hear, but I don't know for sure as I've given up buying things. We're in a recession. We're hunkering down.

As we bring this book to a close, it's best to remember how we found ourselves sitting around one day, minding our own business, thinking things were just hunky-dory, and then poof. There goes everything. Your job. Your money. Vanished just like that. They say our economy has lost something like $50 trillion or zillion dollars—whatever the new word is for a boatload of money. It's hard not to get depressed thinking about the mess we find ourselves in.

We need to have a brief discussion on how best to proceed going forward. The best way to avoid falling into a bucket of sheep dip is to avoid being around sheep. To do that you need to plan ahead.

I know, I know, there is nothing in the world more boring and confusing than trying to plan for the future.

"If I do this, then that will happen. If I do that, then this will happen. "But what about if I do…?"
Pass me a beer. I'm getting dizzy thinking about it.

[212]

Conversations such as this are taking place all over the country today. The herd is panicking. It's trying to figure out how we got here; what to do now; what to do next. There's enough angst floating around to sink the spirits of the chronically upbeat.

How do you plan ahead for crooks and thieves and scoundrels? You need to think and live more like a Vermonter. We've dealt with crooks, thieves, scoundrels, encyclopedia salesmen, tourists, skiers, farmers, pikers, scalpers, drug dealers, kooks, check bouncers, transients, slimeballs, developers/land rapists, terrorists, creeps—you name it. If they're out there, they passed through Vermont at one time or another. It makes life somewhat much more interesting, but it is best to keep your distance when you run into one of these characters.

This helps explain why Vermonters can be somewhat standoffish when first met. They might seem unfriendly to the untrained eye, but that's because we're busy planning. We plan constantly. We plan for the worst each second of each minute of each hour of each day of, because we're used to things not being all that great, followed by the prospects of becoming much worse.

If you have any doubt about this, you need only to talk to maple syrup producer/car salesman/auto-body repairman/mechanic, Bob Bushee. Like most Vermonters he's hedging his bets. No point in having one job that you could lose in the blink of an eye. No sir, he has three or four or five; hard to keep track. He puts up, on average, about 1,000 gallons of maple syrup each spring. If he put up 10,000 gallons next spring and you were to ask him how the season was, he'd say, "Not great. Better'n last year, but not great."

Why would he say that if he put up ten times more syrup than the previous year? Two answers to that question. First, he's a Vermonter and Vermonters can't comprehend the idea of a "good year." There are simply varying degrees of bad years. The same is true with farming, skiing, or pretty much anything else. As was stated in the beginning of this book, Vermont has considered itself to have been in a recession since around 1790, shortly after the

[213]

"good years"—the ones immediately after the Revolutionary War. Things picked up in later years for the rest of the country, but not so in Vermont. We had no idea how lucky we were to be until hundreds of years later. That is real planning ahead even if no one knew it at the time.

A handful of Vermonters opined at the great gains that the rest of the world was experiencing, hoping that one day the wave of success would reach Vermont. The rest knew better. They knew that there was only so much air you can put in a balloon before it pops. It wasn't all that hard to see it coming.

Through no conscience effort we tend to look at the world as described by Kris Kristofferson in a song he wrote a long time ago, "If you ain't got nothing, you got nothing to lose."

Thus, the key to success and to surviving a recession is to ensure that you have nothing, or at best, darned little. There you have it. It took a great deal of foresight and planning to figure this all out and fortunately for you, here it is all written out in this book.

Presumably, you would not have come to this conclusion on your own. You'd keep right on trying to get more and more money so that you could give it to some investor-type and then end up right behind the average Vermonter—only worse. You'd be depressed to be where you are. The Vermonter would be as content as ever.

Planning to start off flat broke saves a lot of time that can be invested doing other things. Things that are really important, like finding someone who really loves you for who you are, not because you have a lot of money. Somebody who will tolerate your quirks unconditionally. Someone who thinks that the most important thing that a human being can do is to see who can walk on railroad tracks the longest without having to step off on the ties.

Money and wealth are not all that important. Spend a little more time reflecting on what makes a life worth living. If you conclude that it's money, well best of luck to you.

If you can see that life is more about relationships, love, and beauty; the way the sky changes color every second at the end of the day; the way the deer looks at you when startled; the way your friends like you and your foes respect you; then you may just end up the richest man in the world. How cool is that?

The Best Laid Plans

It's going to be a record-breaking hot day on this lovely Saturday at the end of April. Eighty-six degrees is pretty hot for just about any time in Vermont, say anything about April. Hot, sunny days really lay on the old pressure. It becomes immediately evident how much work needs to be done. Planning becomes all encompassing.

I find myself standing in freshly fertilized and tilled soil for the thirtieth time. Over the years Alison and I have sketched out various designs as to how we want to lay out the garden. Should the rows go north and south, or east and west? Raised beds? Starburst rows emanating from the center?

Crops must be rotated so as not to drain the soil of its much-needed nutrients. Where were the tomatoes last year? Right over there on the west side of the garden. No, they were more toward the flower garden. We spend a lot of time discussing the various options of laying out the garden. I believe this is why they made coffee. Notwithstanding the fact that I am a decaf coffee drinker, there are really very few things more enjoyable in life than standing and looking at the clean slate of dirt and wondering, no, make that "planning" what will go where while drinking a cup of coffee.

A few years ago I bought a small, used rototiller. Prior to that we had always mulched the garden with everything from black plastic (way back in the early days, before we realized what a waste of a nonrenewable resource that was) to straw; the latter being the better option. When using a tiller, one must plan very carefully as it needs a lot of room to move. The barren rows of dirt look manageable now. Maneuvering around at this stage is no problem.

[215]

But "now" is not the problem. Tomorrow is when the problem arrives.

Tomorrow the tomato plants not yet planted will be six feet high and hanging all over everything. The area designated for squash, which seems perfectly adequate as we stand there sipping coffee, will shrink as the giant leaves and accommodating vines wind there way through the potatoes and beans, crushing them along the way. Maybe we should plan to give them a little more space this year. Figuring this out now could save a lot of "could'a, would'a, should'a" talk in August.

In the blink of an eye, August will be here and if the past is any indicator at all of the future, then I expect we'll be mumbling and grumbling about how we "could'a" done this or "should'a" done that.

With the soil turned, the rows staked out and the raised bed for the lettuce installed, it is hard not to be overcome by anxiety of what will be. Hopefully, everything that we did on this glorious day will make things right down the road.

If only we put as much thought into our own future as we do into that of our garden. There were things on the horizon that were pretty clear. Things like over consumption, greed, power (both political and energy wise), a selfish lifestyle. Over the past two (out of how many?) generations, we somehow either decided or were told that the limited resources on this planet were unlimited, so that was how we chose to live; like everything that is will always be.

Then, one day we learn that the company that helped us to win WWII, General Motors, is on the verge of bankruptcy. While sitting at the kitchen table reading the text on our laptop, we learn that institutional newspapers are on their way out, apparently grabbing right on to the coattails of Lehman Bros. and half of our banks. The nonexistent newspapers enlighten us to the fact that all of those million-dollar homes purchased over the last few years were only worth about half of the purchase price. Guys who were only last year pulling down some major big bucks are now out of work and joining the PTA, since they are the ones responsible for taking care of the kids while Mom works.

It was devastating to discover that a former head of the New York Stock Exchange, America's more credible financial institution, did a most incredible thing—set up a Ponzi scheme that stole $50-plus billion of other people's money. He ruined lives for money.

The best-laid plans are always subject to outside forces. Try as you might, something will inevitably occur that will alter your plans. That's life. But when you can see it coming, when you know what will happen, you can't blame it on others. It's your own fault.

Your best bet is to take a second look at the distance between those rows. If you think they are not far enough apart, now is the time to widen them just a little bit more. Better give that tiller plenty of room, because it's unforgiving when making a turn. Pour yourself another cup of coffee and spend just a few more minutes planning. It might save you some regrets down the road.
April 26, 2009

Chapter 25

Wrap It Up

Let's take a moment to recap just what the heck it was I was hoping to accomplish by sitting in front of my computer all this time. OK, first of all I was kidding. This really is an autobiography in a thinly veiled disguise as a guide to surviving a recession. That said, though, there are some pretty darn good tips here.

It was also a good chance to tell those friends of Joe Allen's a little bit about Vermont. I hate to use the overused cliché that Vermont is a unique place, but it is. It's also a mysterious place; a place that now has a variety of folks. Many people living in the southern end of the state have relocated here from other places. These folks tend to not want to go much further than, say, Dorset, for fear of Indian attacks. They need to know that it's safe to go out.

I had some New York City friends who moved up here years ago. I asked if they spent much time in the woods. They looked at me like I had suddenly become a vampire.

"Oh my god, no! I'm afraid to go into the woods." Guess they didn't know that the woods of Vermont are the safest place on planet earth.

Like the rest of the world, this place is changing, but it still has descendants spawned from those rugged flatlanders of yore; enough so that the outside world is, if not frightened of us, at least a little puzzled by us. It's still the whitest state in the nation yet the first state to support the nation's first black president.

It is predominately a socially liberal, fiscally conservative state that has large Democratic majorities in both its House and Senate, yet has elected a Republican governor and lieutenant governor. It's an enigma to just about everyone—even some natives.

It's a state of many firsts. It was the first state to ban billboards, enact bottle bill legislation and land-use development laws, and recognize the rights of gays and lesbians to marry without a court

[219]

order. We don't particularly care who you are or what you do as long as you keep to yourself and are nice to people.

At the time this book was written our nation, and the world, appears to be cascading into a financial abyss, although the Obama stimulus package did pass, so there could be hope. Hope, that is, for the rest of you.

For Vermont it probably won't make much difference. Vermonters have always lived like they are in a recession. Few who were born here and choose to remain here ever get money rich. In that race they come in last and don't mind all that much.

In the end it may just be that they are the world's wealthiest people. They are rich in heritage. They are rich in friendship and family. They are rich in stories (thanks to those of you who have moved up here and provided us with endless material). They are made wealthy by the rising and setting sun. They are made wealthy by a blizzard lasting for days, trapping them in their homes with no power, thus allowing them to remember, if only for a moment, what life was like for their ancestors. A good spring flood provides us with rich conversation at our general stores and diners until the hot days of summer arrive. The weather binds us as tightly together as does our DNA.

The lessons learned growing up in this small state should be shared with the country so that all of America can understand that the closer we are to each other, the closer we are to the ground; the closer we are to the past, the richer our lives will be.

Money is a tool. Without money you couldn't afford to buy a car. Without a car, you wouldn't be able to fly off the snowy road with your all-season tires and get stuck in a ditch. Without getting stuck in a ditch, Vermonters are unnecessarily deprived of a good story that will carry them on for weeks, maybe even months, if it's a good old-fashioned, right-up-to-the-doors, stuck-in-a-ditch deal.

Money should be seen as a means to help you live, not the reason to live. Living is the reason to live. John Lennon said it best, "Life is what happens to you while you're busy making other plans." It would seem as though by now we should have figured out that the best way to get through life is to just live it. It's only hard if we make it so.

We unnecessarily fill our backpacks with rocks. Much of life's burdens are those that we impose upon ourselves. We have successfully transformed what was once a pretty peaceful existence into a most complicated affair. Live in a state (or state of mind) with a slower pace and you'll come to see life in a different way. You will learn of things that truly make one rich.

Things like the changing of the color of leaves, watching a mayfly land on the back of your hand in early spring, or simply walking on railroad tracks with the one you love and the one who loves you. The wonders of the world are right there in front of you, but only if you are able to see them. You must first understand what truly makes you rich. Once you do, it will be that wealth that will carry you successfully to the end of your days.

If the recession has wiped you out, think of it as an opportunity to come here and spend what few bucks you have left at our local stores and farmer's markets. You will be a little poorer but you also will be wealthier from the friends and experiences money can't buy. You will boost our local economy and help to keep us going for another hundred years, just like we have for the past two hundred and fifty—just barely—just fine.

You may even come to like this way of life, too. If so, you won't give a rat's backside if we're in a recession or not because you'll be living life.

In good times or bad, life is always worth living. It doesn't really matter if we are in a recession or a boom time. The only thing that matters is how you live and how you love. It can be great or not. It's up to you. Make the most of it. What do you have to lose?

[221]

Again, special thanks to Joe Allen, who had no idea that thirty years ago his words would mean a lot to me. Sorry it took so long, Joe. Thanks for the kick in the pants.

"That mosquito is so big it could stand flat-footed and fuck a chicken."
James P. Stannard, Sr.

This quote was overheard by my grandfather, John Stannard, when my father who, as a youngster, was working in a ditch. The bug in question landed on my father's arm while he was digging. His father/boss was standing on the ground overlooking the ditch with a customer at his side when my dad felt compelled to share his observations.

Most likely, my grandfather, a plumber who always wore a black suit and tie, spit shined shoes, and a fedora, was not amused. Children have a way of doing that to parents…which is as it should be.

If you can make it through parenting, a recession ain't no big deal.

The End
Or
The beginning, depending upon whether or not you have a
Vermont perspective

The Author -
Bob Stannard is an eighth generational Vermonter. He has served
in the Vermont legislature. He's worked as a logger, mowed
lawns, sold commercial real estate and has lobbied the Vermont
legislature on many important issues.

In his spare time he is a Harmonica player/Blues singer/song
writer. His musical talent has led him to perform with some great
Bluesmen including BB King, Mark Hummel, David Maxwell,
John Hammond, Louisiana Red and many others. Running into
Jerry Portnoy at a Bar didn't hurt either.

He has released two CDs his most recent; "Bob Stannard &
Friends - LIVE at the Black Door", can be purchased from his
website: www.bobstannard.com. For that matter you can get this
book there, too! But since you're standing here with this book in
your hand save yourself the trouble and just wonder over to the
check-out counter and pay the nice person there.

He is also a columnist for the Bennington Banner and as if all this
isn't enough to qualify him to be on the federal government's list
of "Most Dangerous People" he is a practicing Martial Artist.

Bob Stannard lives in Manchester with his wife, Alison. They
have two grown children, Meredith Hairston and Wesley Stannard.

This is Bob's first book. If you
buy another copy for a friend he
promises to write another
second. OK, just buy this one
and we'll leave it at that.

Contact Bob by email:
bob@bobstannard.com